The National Rivers Authority

WATER: NATURE'S PRECIOUS RESOURCE

AN ENVIRONMENTALLY SUSTAINABLE WATER RESOURCES DEVELOPMENT STRATEGY FOR ENGLAND AND WALES

National Rivers Authority
March 1994

LONDON: HMSO

The National Rivers Authority

ACKNOWLEDGEMENTS

The National Rivers Authority (NRA) acknowledges the help and advice given in the preparation of this strategy by the many bodies and organisations with interests in the environment and water industry, including:

British Waterways
Confederation of British Industry
Council for the Protection of Rural England
Country Landowners Association
Countryside Commission
Countryside Council for Wales
Department of Environment
Department of Trade and Industry
English Nature
Farmers Union of Wales
Inland Waterways Association
Ministry of Agriculture, Fisheries and Food
National Farmers Union
National Power Plc
Office of Water Services
Power Gen Plc
Royal Society for Nature Conservation
Royal Society for the Protection of Birds
SERPLAN
U.K. Irrigation Association
Water Service Companies
Water Companies
Water Services Association
Water Companies Association
Welsh Office

The NRA also acknowledges the valuable assistance provided by its main consultants Sir William Halcrow & Partners Limited and the contributions from the supporting consultants Howard Humphreys and Partners Limited.

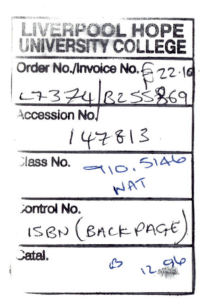

CONTENTS

TABLES

FIGURES

The National Rivers Authority

APPENDIX 1:

Local Resource Development Options Included in the Marginal Demand Analysis.

APPENDIX 2:

Key Strategic Resource Options and Transfer Links.

A2.1   River Severn to River Thames Transfer.

A2.2   South West Oxfordshire Reservoir.

A2.3   River Severn to River Trent Transfer.

A2.4   Canal Transfer to the Thames and Anglian Regions.

A2.5   East Anglian Reservoir

A2.6   Unsupported River Trent to Anglian Transfer

A2.7   Birmingham Rising Groundwater.

APPENDIX 3:

Environmental Implications of Key Strategic Resource Options and Transfer Links.

A3.1   Introduction.

A3.2   Role of Environmental Assessment.

A3.3   Method of Assessing Environmental Implications.

A3.4   Criteria for Assessing Environmental Impact.

A3.5   Comparison of Strategic Options.

A3.6   Key Issues

A3.7   Further Studies

APPENDIX 4:

Summary of Research and Development Projects Relating to Environmental Economics

EXECUTIVE SUMMARY

OBJECTIVES

The overall aim of this strategy is to develop an environmentally sustainable water resources development strategy for England and Wales.

Within this overall aim, specific objectives are:

- to establish whether major water resources developments are required over the next 30 years;
- if so which schemes are likely to be most acceptable;
- to set out the actions which need to be taken to improve confidence in future decisions.

INTRODUCTION

In March 1992 the National Rivers Authority (NRA) published its 'Water Resources Development Strategy Discussion Document', which reported upon the balance between the need for water resources and their availability across England and Wales. It also took a first look at the possible need for additional water resource developments and the options which could be implemented if needed.

Since 1992 work has been carried out to establish and refine the components of an environmentally sustainable water resources strategy which aims at ensuring that legitimate needs for abstraction are met in a way which will be environmentally sustainable.

The concept of sustainable development has been an integral part of the Government's policy and practice in recent years and builds on the widely accepted definition given in the 1987 Report of the World Commission on Environment and Development - the Brundtland Report - that sustainable development is:

> "...development that meets the needs of the present without compromising the ability of future generations to meet their own needs."

In its widest context sustainable development includes environmental, economic and social considerations. From the NRA's perspective the concepts of sustainability are concentrated upon the water environment and relate to the NRA's mission to protect and improve the environment.

In preparing the strategy, specific consideration has been given to:

- the existing balance of resources and demands;
- future demands for public water supply, industry and agriculture;
- the need to improve 'low flow rivers' resulting from excessive abstraction;
- the selection of water resource options needed to meet justified needs.

The selection of water resources options for meeting future demand has been based on environmental, cost and other considerations such as the time needed to fully investigate and promote new schemes, which can be 20 years or more. In the longer term it is anticipated that the final scheme selection will eminate from a full economic analysis, which includes quantification of environmental aspects.

In arriving at the possible need for strategic water resource development it has been assumed that where local options exist, they would be developed before a strategic option. The national strategy has therefore examined the marginal demands which may need to be met from schemes which tend to involve the transfer of water from one river basin to another or which are relatively large in scale and impact.

Climate change could influence the water resources development strategy. However given current uncertainties in the validity of some predictions, it is thought that there is insufficient evidence available to allow assumptions about climate change to be incorporated at the present time.

POLICY FRAMEWORK

The NRA has developed and refined a range of key policies and concepts which are essential to an environmentally sustainable water resources strategy. Foremost amongst these are:

- *Sustainable Development* - The NRA's main concern is for environmental sustainability. This implies that there should be no long-term systematic deterioration in the water environment due to water resource development and water use.

- *Precautionary Principle* - where significant environmental damage may occur, but knowledge on the matter is incomplete, decisions made and measures implemented should err on the side of caution.

- *Demand Management* - The management of the total quantity of water taken from sources of supply using measures to control waste and consumption.

Within these concepts lie a range of more specific policies, notably:

- requiring water companies to achieve economic levels of leakage and metering before new abstraction licences are granted for strategic developments;

- the promotion of water efficiency by industry, commerce, agriculture and use in the home;

- where possible, redistribution of water resources, rather than the development of new sources;

- favouring schemes which lead to an improvement in the water environment;

- favouring schemes which meet the widest interests;

- protecting and improving the quality of water resources.

THE NRA ROLE

The NRA is the licensing authority for water abstraction. It has a statutory duty to secure the proper use of water resources which includes:

- assessing the need for new developments;

- ensuring that the most appropriate schemes are licensed, taking into account the environmental impact of new developments and the impact on existing users.

The financing, promotion and development of new schemes would normally be the concern of the main beneficiaries. The NRA will however ensure that the needs of smaller abstractors are not overlooked.

The initiative for developing new schemes will rest with:

- a water company or consortium of water companies;

- other private sector investors.

DEMANDS AND RESOURCES

PUBLIC WATER SUPPLY Particular attention has been given to the identification of possible future public water supply needs since this is the largest demand of any purpose.

The principal factors which have an influence on public water supply demand are:

- population growth and household size;

- consumption per person;

- the method of charging for water services and the price level adopted;

- levels of leakage from distribution systems and consumers' plumbing;

- water consumption of household appliances and their level of ownership;

- the level of economic activity;

- gardening habits.

In the past, it has generally been the practice to develop new resources to keep ahead of the rise in demand. Now, however, it is considered appropriate to identify what steps can be taken to control demand to see if new developments are really essential.

Three demand scenarios for public water supply have therefore been considered which take demand management factors into account.

● *High* - the growth in demand assuming relatively high rates of growth in domestic and non-domestic consumption and no (or negligible) increase in current demand management activity.

● *Medium* - the growth in demand assuming a moderate growth in domestic and non-domestic consumption, limited domestic metering and reduced leakage.

● *Low* - the growth in demand assuming moderate growth in domestic consumption, no increase in non-household consumption, moderate domestic metering and further reduced leakage.

These scenarios describe the possible range of demand for the next 30 years.

RESOURCES AND DEMAND BALANCE

Currently there is a surplus in public water supply resources. However, in 30 years time, given the possible range of increases in public water supply demand a supply deficit could occur in most areas.

The development of small water resource schemes local to specific areas of demand will go some way towards addressing the potential deficits. These so called 'local options' are numerous but will nevertheless require rigorous examination on environmental and economic grounds before they can be developed. However if all such local options were to be developed then under the medium and high demand scenarios the outstanding deficits in water resources would require strategic developments to redress the balance. If demand followed the low scenario, then no strategic developments would be required.

A summary of the growth in public water supply demand is shown opposite.

Summary of Public Water Supply Demand

Demand Scenario	Average Growth in average Public Water Supply Demand to 2021 (expressed as % of 1991 demand)	Potential Shortfall in Supply Ml/d (assuming 'local' resource options are developed)
High • No (or negligible) demand management • High growth in domestic consumption • High growth in non-domestic consumption	25%	1110
Medium • Some demand management • Moderate growth in domestic consumption • Moderate growth in non-domestic consumption	10%	142
Low • Increasing demand management • Moderate growth in domestic consumption • No growth in non-domestic consumption	2%	0

DEMAND MANAGEMENT

One of the main differences between the three demand scenarios is the extent of demand management. The modest adoption of the key demand management measures of domestic metering and leakage control has a significant effect on the requirement for new resource developments.

This effect is so marked that a proper consideration of demand management measures must be a primary element in a sustainable water resources strategy.

ALLEVIATION OF LOW FLOWS

The NRA is committed to alleviating the problem of low flow rivers caused by excessive abstraction. These problems were generally caused by abstractions authorised by Licences of Right granted under the Water Resources Act 1963. A total of some 300 Ml/d has been taken from the existing available resources to account for the loss of yield in varying or revoking these licences to improve these problem rivers.

INDUSTRY, AGRICULTURE AND POWER GENERATION

Of the other significant demands on water resources, namely industry, agriculture and power generation (mainly for cooling), only agriculture has been forecast to show any significant increase in the next 30 years. The majority of agricultural use of water is for spray irrigation, principally in East Anglia.

Although agricultural use of water is only 1% of total water demand, abstraction is concentrated during dry periods and can have a significant impact on water resources. The most likely increase in demand for agriculture has been estimated at around 1.7% per annum to 2001 and 1% per annum thereafter to 2021.

The main options for meeting such needs are considered to be:

● investment in new resources:
 - on-farm winter fill storage by individual farmers;

- medium scale local development by co-operative ventures;
- shares in strategic developments.

- management initiatives:
  - cash payments between farmers to 'buy out' water rights;
  - pooling licences by groups of farmers;
  - improved management of resources;
  - incentive charges to control demand;
  - reallocation of resources through tradeable permits.

Some of these initiatives could only be introduced if there is a change in the controlling legislation.

- improved efficiency:
  - improved irrigation techniques in terms of time of application;
  - improvements in operating practices and systems.

THE DEVELOPMENT OPTIONS AND THEIR ENVIRONMENTAL EFFECTS

DEVELOPMENT OPTIONS

A number of possible options for meeting the marginal demands have been considered in the development of the strategy. Some unusual options have been reviewed such as desalination, direct effluent re-use and water by ship or in towed flexible bags. These have not been taken forward within the strategy development for a variety of reasons, but mainly due to high capital and operating costs, public health concerns or risks associated with uncertain technology.

Preference has been given to the more conventional options which include:

- South West Oxfordshire reservoir;

- East Anglian reservoir;

- partial redeployment of Vyrnwy reservoir to regulate the River Severn;

- enlargement of Craig Goch reservoir to regulate the River Severn or River Wye;

- transfers from the River Wye or River Severn to the River Thames;

- transfers from the River Trent to East Anglia;

- transfers from the River Severn to the River Trent;

- transfers utilising the canal network.

ENVIRONMENTAL ASSESSMENT

A preliminary environmental overview has been completed to identify the environmental implications for each of the possible strategic developments. The purpose of the assessment is to highlight the key environmental issues which may favour or discriminate against particular options.

Some of the key issues arising from the preliminary assessment relate to the:-

● effect on flora and fauna of mixing water of different chemistries;

● transfer of species and diseases between catchments;

● loss of terrestrial habitats due to reservoir construction;

● effect of changed river flows on fish movement;

● possible environmental benefits which can be obtained from specific developments.

For a number of the strategic options, the potential environmental impact will be dependent upon the size of scheme required which in turn will be determined by the demand which needs to be met. It is an inescapable fact however, that all reservoir construction and inter-basin transfers will have some impact on the aquatic environment. If a policy of 'no change' is seriously proposed, it would mean that no development could be supported. The central issue for the NRA therefore, is to question the need for the development and the scale and significance of any environmental change which may occur.

THE STRATEGY

The key messages emerging from the strategy are that:

● there is a strong possibility that demands can be managed to avoid the need for large scale water resources developments over the next 20 years or so;

● water companies must be required to achieve economic levels of leakage and metering before new abstraction licences are granted for strategic developments;

● the NRA must take a proactive role in promoting water use efficiency in industry, commerce, agriculture and the home;

● environmental considerations will be crucial, where in doubt a precautionary approach should be adopted;

● the attitude of companies to involvement in strategic transfer schemes with other companies as opposed to being in control of their own resources is an important factor;

● early planning of some major resource developments is necessary.

Included within the conclusions of the strategy are the following:

● By far the greatest need for additional water resources, should a High or Medium demand scenario materialise, is in the Thames catchment. Although a new reservoir in the Thames Valley has been proposed, serious consideration still needs to be given to alternative ways of developing a resource to meet a future need. In cost terms a transfer from the River Severn to the River Thames is a possible alternative, but the environmental implications appear to be greater than for a reservoir. A detailed environmental impact study of this option needs to be carried out as soon as possible.

● The partial redeployment of Vyrnwy reservoir, which is currently used as an important good quality gravity supply to the North West has been considered. However, it is not recommended that early plans are developed to redeploy this reservoir for regulation of the River Severn. Nevertheless, partial Vyrnwy redeployment would appear to offer a good contingency source in that it could be brought on line relatively quickly if the need arises, provided supplies within North West region could be switched to make up any supply shortfall from Vyrnwy reservoir.

● A new resource for East Anglia will be needed under the High and Medium demand scenarios. Although analysis has so far been based upon the Great Bradley reservoir location, investigations are at an advanced stage concerning an alternative site on the fens. The results of these investigations are not known at present, but early selection of a preferred option is essential.

● British Waterways (BW) have undertaken engineering studies of possible canal transfers from the Midlands to East Anglia and the Thames area. Large scale transfers via the canals are more expensive than other options mainly because of the cost of bringing spare water to the canals (eg, via a possible River Severn to River Trent transfer). Transfers via canals would not be without environmental problems but, providing these could be overcome, it is possible that they could be used for small scale transfers.

WAY FORWARD

There is much more work to be done and the strategy identifies a number of specific proposals for the next 5 years. The most important of these are:

● to give renewed impetus to the promotion of water efficiency;

● to address environmental issues in readiness for new developments should demand management prove ineffective;

● to give particular attention to the agricultural need for water, especially spray irrigation in eastern England;

● to review the feasibility, cost and environmental impact of local schemes and to compare them with the strategic options.

1. INTRODUCTION

The principal aim of the water resources function of the National Rivers Authority (NRA) is to "manage water resources to achieve the right balance between the needs of the environment and those of the abstractors" (NRA, 1993). The specific objective of this report is to establish the components of an environmentally sustainable water resources strategy. It will consider whether major water resources development is required over the next 30 years and if so which schemes are likely to be most acceptable. The strategy is a statement at a point in time in what will be a continuing process of updating and refinement. Many uncertainties exist in the planning of future water resources and within the strategy the opportunity is taken to identify unresolved questions and the work needed to answer them.

Water resources have to be developed to be able to meet abstraction requirements during drought years and the end of the drought of the late 1980s and early 1990s has not altered the need to develop a strategy. Experience of the recent drought has been beneficial in that it has increased understanding of the stresses placed on water resources schemes and has generally confirmed the integrity of existing systems. It has also highlighted the problems associated with low flows and the agricultural need for water.

The strategy deals only with the possible need for new water resources following the implementation of 'local' schemes. These so called 'local schemes' have not been defined in specific terms, but normally they are located within the catchment from which the water is abstracted, are of a relatively small size and would be developed where a strategic option would not appear to be a serious alternative. Hence the national strategy has examined the margin of demand which may need to be met from schemes which tend to involve transfer of water from one basin to another or which are relatively large in scale and impact.

Planning of water resources is also being carried out by the NRA on a regional basis and this concentrates more upon local options and takes greater account of immediate needs. The preparation of regional and national water resources plans has been integrated to ensure that the broad high level approach adopted in the national study is compatible with the more detailed approach used in regional work.

Within the context of this strategy planning and modelling work has been carried out on the basis of 10 regions within England and Wales. These areas have been chosen on water resources grounds and equate to the 10 regional NRA boundaries which existed until recently. The NRA is now based on 8 regions which involved the merger of Northumbria and Yorkshire regions and of South West and Wessex regions.

The NRA's Water Resources Development Strategy Discussion Document, (NRA, 1992a) was published in March 1992 and stimulated widespread comment from many organisations. These included environmental groups, water supply companies, research groups, manufacturers, representatives of abstractors and many individuals who put forward their own views and suggestions on how water resources should be managed and protected for future generations.

The responses received have provided a valuable insight into the concerns of people who demand a healthy water environment and of those who have a responsibility for providing water supplies to their customers or who use water for other purposes. The views expressed are gratefully acknowledged and have played a significant part in shaping this strategy.

A number of reports have been published over the last two years which have had an important bearing on this strategy (DoE, 1992a; POST 1993; Rees & Williams, 1993). All these papers have highlighted the opportunities for demand management which this strategy examines on a national basis.

The NRA's Water Resources Development Strategy addresses:

● the policy framework and criteria for an environmentally sustainable development strategy;

● the existing balance of resources and demands;

● future demand scenarios based on alternative assumptions regarding growth and demand management;

● resource development options;

● environmental assessments;

● financial analysis;

● alternative strategies for sources and transfers to meet possible demands.

These issues are discussed in more detail in the following sections together with the financing, promotion and development of new resources.

Not all regions of the NRA have a possible need for new strategic supplies. The strategy concentrates on the need to meet marginal demands for water, after taking account of the scale of existing resources, potential local options and the possible growth in the demand for water. The main NRA regions considered as potential beneficiaries of strategic resource development are Thames, Anglian, Severn-Trent and the Wessex area of the South West region.

Climate change could have an impact upon any water resources development strategy. At present there are many uncertainties regarding the possible impacts of climate change, especially in the confidence associated with prediction. The NRA is keeping a close eye on the results of climate change research but at the present time it does not believe there is sufficient evidence to make specific allowance for it in its water resources strategy.

2. POLICY FRAMEWORK FOR A DEVELOPMENT STRATEGY

The NRA is responsible for the management of water resources in England and Wales. As the Guardians of the Water Environment, the NRA is committed to ensuring that proper use is secured through a long term strategy which will sustain water resources for generations to come. The efficient use of water resources combined with sensitivity towards the environment is considered to be the most appropriate approach towards sustaining a healthy water environment as well as an acceptable balance between environmental and other demands for water. Overall, the strategy is guided by a balanced adoption of three fundamental principles: economic efficiency, sustainability and precaution.

After rapid growth in the 1960s the demand for public water supply has increased rather less during the 1970s and 1980s, as shown in Figure 1. Until recently, the future provision of water resources has generally been demand led, but as available water resources become increasingly utilised it is clear that a more efficient approach to balancing demands and supply must be developed in the long term to protect and improve the water environment.

Figure 1

SUPPLY AND DEMAND FOR PUBLIC WATER SUPPLY - 1961 TO 2021

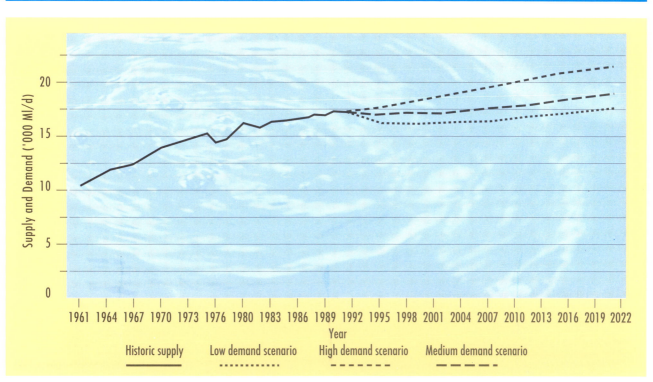

With water resources in some parts of the country already approaching full utilisation, there is no room for complacency and demand for water by all users will need to be more efficiently managed over the years and decades to come. Where legitimate demands for new water resource developments are justified, then only environmentally acceptable schemes should be developed.

Significant impact on water demand can arise from selective metering of domestic consumers, improved leakage control, more efficient water using appliances and better water management by agricultural and industrial users, encouraged by appropriate tariffs for abstraction and discharge. The combined effects of these measures need to be evaluated not just in economic terms, but also in terms of their impact on the environment.

The NRA's strategy is formulated from policies based on principles of sustainability, aimed at protection and enhancement of the water environment, while ensuring the availability of essential supplies as efficiently as possible. Some of the key policies include:

● applying principles and criteria of sustainability to the water environment, taking a precautionary approach in areas of uncertainty.

● reviewing levels of abstraction in terms of sustainability and proper use.

● promoting and encouraging the efficient use of water including:

   - support for selective domestic metering in areas where water resources are under stress and where the development of additional resources is difficult to achieve without harm to the environment;

   - the need for water companies to evaluate the economics of selective domestic metering as an option for delaying the need for new water resource development before issuing new licences;

   - the need for water companies to demonstrate that steps have been taken to reduce leakage to acceptable levels before issuing a licence for new resource developments;

   - promotion of more efficient use of water by industry and agriculture, through the use of water audits, demonstration projects and advice.

● securing operational safeguards where necessary to protect or improve the environment where new schemes involve reservoir storage, river regulation, augmentation or transfer between rivers.

● seeking to ensure that abstractors develop sufficient resources to meet their reasonable needs without frequent drought order applications, which, if granted would adversely impact on the aquatic environment.

● protecting and improving the quality of water resources.

● favouring schemes which:

   - allow augmentation of river flows at times of drought or provide benefit to low flow rivers;

   - make use of under-utilised water resources, rather than development of new sources, including reallocation between companies;

   - have net environmental benefits such as the provision of releases which improve the water environment;

- avoid piecemeal development, except where this is relatively small development to meet local demand;

- benefit all classes of abstractor;

- make use of development opportunities within the local catchment in preference to inter-basin transfers where the overall impacts and costs are judged to be similar;

- are economically efficient;

- return treated effluent of a high standard at or near the point of abstraction or at a site which will augment other stressed resources.

● seeking to protect the interests of other abstractors who are not specific beneficiaries of a particular water resources development and, where appropriate, entering into agreement with the developer to secure a portion of the source for use by such abstractors. In these circumstances the NRA would seek to recover its costs from the beneficiaries.

The strategy does not give significant attention to groundwater development because in many parts of the country groundwater resources are already being fully utilised. However, there are some areas where further groundwater could be developed for local use to meet legitimate water needs in an economic way. The principle of sustainability requires not only that long term abstraction should be less then average recharge, but also that much less is available for abstraction because an allowance should be made for rivers and wetlands dependent upon that recharge. Key aspects of the NRA's approach to further groundwater development are that:

● river support boreholes may be required to guarantee river flows for abstraction at or near the tidal limits to supply areas where the water is subsequently lost to sea;

● some use of groundwater for irrigation and other non-returning use will be allowed subject to the maintenance of satisfactory river flows;

● where spring and river flows are unacceptably affected, compensation river support pumping will be required to sustain satisfactory minimum flows;

● new boreholes must avoid unacceptable effects on recognised wetlands.

Determining the potential conflict between the needs of abstractors and those of the environment is not a straightforward process and a number of issues need to be taken into account. Future decision making in water resources will be conditioned by criteria for environmental, social and economic sustainability. The need to protect the water environment will be given priority where the capacity for water resources is judged to be at or near its limit, applying the precautionary principle where appropriate. Economic instruments may also be developed to assist with the realisation of an environmentally sustainable water resources development strategy. Effective regulation will however remain essential to protect critical environmental conditions.

New licences to abstract will only be granted if the NRA is satisfied of the need for new resources following a thorough analysis of demand, the scope for demand management and an appropriate environmental assessment. Where there is still doubt surrounding a particular proposal and any threat to the environment is significant, the application of the precautionary principle could result in:

● abstraction licence applications being rejected or modified;

● licences being time limited;

● conditions being placed on licences so that they are 'fail safe' from an environmental perspective.

The NRA will also support the promotion of local developments, all other things being equal, rather than development remote from the area of demand.

It is sometimes suggested that the NRA should use its water resources powers to control the location of new housing and industry so that new developments can be directed towards those parts of England and Wales which already have spare resources readily available. Government policy is however clear that water resources legislation should not be used for this purpose though the NRA will as a statutory consultee, advise planning authorities on the implications of proposed developments on water resources and other functions for which the NRA has statutory duties. The work that the NRA is doing in relation to the preparation of integrated catchment management plans will play an important part in influencing development. However, adequate advance warning is necessary when major new developments are proposed so that suitable arrangements can be made for new water resources, if they are required.

3. WATER RESOURCES AND DEMANDS

3.1
PUBLIC WATER SUPPLY - PRESENT BALANCE

The demand for public water supply represents about 51% of water abstracted and is the largest demand for any purpose as shown in Figure 2. Resources developed to meet this demand are highly integrated so that in many cases reservoirs, direct river intakes and abstractions from underground can be used conjunctively according to circumstance. These sources can be operated to meet different and often conflicting objectives. Sources could be operated to minimise costs, but this is not always in the best interests of the environment. The NRA must therefore ensure that water companies operate to agreed policies which will protect the environment whilst ensuring continued availability of supplies to meet the legitimate demands of consumers.

The present balance between the resources available to water companies and the current average demand is shown in Figure 3. The data shown in Figure 3 differ to some extent to those shown in the Water Resources Development Strategy Discussion Document which was published in March 1992. The data are now based on recent supply information from the water companies in their July 1993 returns to the Office of Water Services (OFWAT) and on improved estimates of the available yield. For presentational purposes the balance shown is a regional average of the total resources and demands for each company within the region and it is recognised that within a region or an individual company the balance will be distributed unevenly.

Figure 2

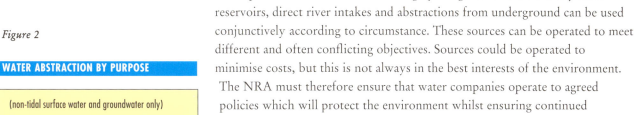

WATER ABSTRACTION BY PURPOSE

(non-tidal surface water and groundwater only)

Public Water Supply
51%

Power Generation Industry
36%

Other Industry
12%

Spray Irrigation and other agriculture
1%

Source: DoE (1992b)

3.2
PUBLIC WATER SUPPLY - FUTURE DEMANDS AND WATER RESOURCE BALANCE

3.2.1
Future Demand Scenarios

The NRA has applied a consistent methodology to produce scenarios of future demand for each Water Service and Water Supply Company in England and Wales.

The method which has been employed is one of component analysis. Demand scenarios for high, medium and low growth are described by the combination of a suite of demand management policy options and broad based assumptions about future growth in demand. These demand scenarios set the range of future consumption between upper and lower limits and therefore indicate an envelope of future demand.

Figure 3

THE PRESENT SURPLUS (PRESENT REGIONAL AVERAGE PUBLIC WATER SUPPLY SURPLUS AS A PERCENTAGE OF 1991 DEMAND)

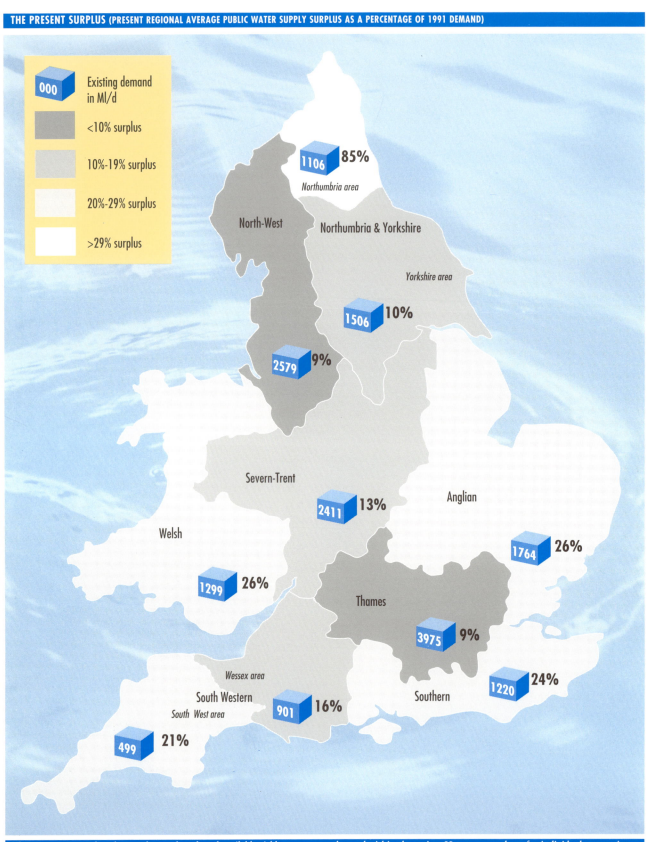

The percentages are based upon the surplus of total available yield over average demand within the region. However, surpluses for individual companies or districts within the region may be higher or lower than the average shown and a surplus in one part of the region may not be transferable to another.

The demand management options and assumptions which are combined to produce the demand scenarios are identified in Table 3.2.1. The scenarios which are built up using these assumptions can be described as follows: (These can be viewed graphically by referring to Figure 1).

● *High* - the growth in demand assuming relatively high rates of growth in domestic and non-domestic consumption and no (or negligible) increase in current demand management activity.

● *Medium* - the growth in demand assuming a moderate growth in domestic and non-domestic consumption, limited domestic metering and reduced leakage.

● *Low* - the growth in demand assuming moderate growth in domestic consumption, no increase in non-household consumption, moderate domestic metering and further reduced leakage.

The data used to produce the demand scenarios have been derived from a number of sources including July 1992 and 1993 company returns to OFWAT and the NRA, as well as information from government departments, external consultants, published papers and consultation with the water companies. Water company forecasts are being updated as part of the OFWAT Asset Management Planning process. These new company forecasts are not expected to be agreed with OFWAT before April 1994.

The principal factors influencing public water supply demand are:

● consumption per person;

● the extent of growth in domestic metering;

● the growth in water efficient appliances and processes;

● the rate of loss of water from company distribution systems and customer properties;

● population growth;

● number of occupants per household;

● underlying level of economic activity.

The NRA believes it has taken a conservative approach to the preparation of its future water company demand scenarios. In particular:

● water company estimates of existing unmetered domestic per capita consumption rates have been used although there are views within the industry that actual consumption is significantly lower in many companies.

● assumed leakage targets are believed to be well within the aspirations of most water companies and total leakage as low as 90 l/prop/day is reported to be targeted by at least one water company.

TABLE 3.2.1

ASSUMPTIONS AND COMBINATIONS WITHIN EACH DEMAND SCENARIO

No.	Assumptions	Assumptions for Each Scenario			
		High	Medium	Low	Broad area of effect
1.	Growth of per capita consumption by compound annual rate of 1%. Per capita figures are constrained to a maximum of 189 l/h/d. Existing per capita consumption from returns to OFWAT in 1993 for 1992 consumption.	■			Per Capita Consumption Growth
2.	Growth of per capita consumption by compound annual percentage rates derived from Binnie & Herrington, (1992). Per capita figures are constrained to a maximum of 180 l/h/d. Existing per capita consumption from returns to OFWAT in 1993 for 1992 consumption.		■	■	
3.	Growth in metered and unmetered non-household consumption by compound annual rate of 0.75% (for all water supply companies).	■			Commercial Growth
4.	Growth in metered and unmetered non-household consumption by compound annual rate of 0.5% (for all companies).		■		
5.	No growth in metered and unmetered non-household consumption above 1991 levels.			■	
6.	No increase in the proportion of domestic metered properties subject to metering above 1991 levels (for all companies). Existing metered properties PCC not reduced by 10% in recognition of the uncertainty associated with such a reduction. Assumed leakage reductions of 30 l/prop/day to account for decreased SPL in existing metered properties.	■			Metering
7.	For companies in Anglian, Severn-Trent, Southern, Thames and Wessex regions 15% of domestic properties will have meters by 2021 (starting in 1996, with equal phasing each year) leading to a 10% reduction in per capita consumption and a reduction in total treated water losses of 30 l/prop/day to account for reduced SPL in metered properties. Other regions Assumption No.6 applies.		■		
8.	For companies in Anglian, Severn-Trent, Southern, Thames and Wessex regions 30% of domestic properties will have meters by 2006 (ongoing from 1996, with equal phasing each year) leading to a 10% reduction in per capita consumption and a reduction in total treated water losses of 30 l/prop/day to account for reduced SPL in metered properties. Other regions Assumption No.6 applies.			■	
9.	Leakage levels per property held at 1991 levels to simulate the effect of no improvements being made to reduce leakage levels. However, if existing leakage is above 290 l/prop/day then it is reduced to this level at a rate of 10 l/prop/day/yr.	■			Leakage
10.	Leakage reduction achieved affecting a reduction in total treated water losses to the following levels in the companies in the regions indicated:- (rate of reduction is 10 l/prop/day/yr). 140 l/prop/day in Anglian, Severn-Trent, Southern, Thames and Wessex; 220 l/prop/day in other regions.		■		
11.	Leakage targets achieved effecting a reduction in total treated water losses to the following levels in the companies in the regions indicated:- (rate of reduction is 20 l/prop/day/yr). 120 l/prop/day in Anglian, Severn-Trent, Southern, Thames and Wessex; 200 l/prop/day in other regions.			■	

Notes: - PCC is Per capita consumption
- SPL is Supply pipe leakage (customer's responsibility)
■ Denotes assumption adopted for the scenario

● growth rates in domestic consumption are based on the views of nationally recognised experts. These rates of growth have been increased for the high scenario.

● domestic meter penetration scenarios are relatively modest being applied only in the South, Central and South East parts of England. They range from no increase in the degree of existing penetration for the High demand scenario, 15% penetration for the Medium demand scenario to 30% for the Low scenario. Savings from metering at 10% are in line with the results of the National Metering Trials. However, twice this saving in consumption has been reported for trials on the Isle of Wight.

The range of percentage increases in regional demand in relation to present demand under the NRA scenarios is shown in Figure 4.

The range between the High and Low demand scenarios demonstrates the significant impact that different basic assumptions make on the need for additional water resources. There are doubts however concerning the actual long term levels of savings which will arise from the implementation of demand management measures and careful monitoring will be required to determine realistic levels. However, the effect of demand management on the need for additional water resources is so marked that it is clear that proper consideration of demand management measures must be a key element in the development of a water resources strategy.

3.2.2
Demand Management

Demand management is the management of the total quantity of water abstracted from a source of supply using measures to control waste and consumption. It will primarily include leakage control through the use of pressure control valves and the repair and replacement of leaking mains and the control of consumption using meters and appropriate tariffs. These measures are normally within the control of water companies, but others can also help to manage demand within the home by attending to leaks and overflows from domestic fittings and careful garden watering. Industry and agriculture may also introduce improved demand management through the introduction of re-cycling and water efficient technologies.

The assumptions used within this strategy for demand management are set out in Table 3.2.1 and can be seen to assume only modest achievements by water companies. However, there is a significant difference of approximately 2,700 Ml/d in shortfall between the High and Low demand scenarios for 2021. This indicates the considerable scope for demand management measures.

The NRA is committed to the promotion of effective demand management measures since these are not environmentally intrusive and may be economic for water companies and their customers. The NRA Board has stated:

> "Before any new sources are developed, it is essential that the water companies make sure they are doing all they can to reduce leakage and carry out demand management."

Figure 4

THE GROWTH SCENARIOS
(INCREASE IN AVERAGE PUBLIC WATER SUPPLY DEMAND TO 2021 UNDER A RANGE OF DEMAND SCENARIOS EXPRESSED AS % OF 1991 DEMAND)

HIGH
MED
LOW
KEY FOR DEMAND SCENARIOS

Northumbria area
16%
10%
6%

North-West

Northumbria & Yorkshire

Yorkshire area
23%
8%
0%

15%
0%
-6%

Severn-Trent
28%
12%
3%

Anglian
37%
27%
18%

Welsh
18%
5%
-1%

Thames
28%
7%
-2%

Southern
31%
15%
6%

Wessex area
32%
15%
6%

South Western
South West area
43%
27%
19%

The percentages are based on a summation of average demands for the companies in each region.

For demand management to be effective an integrated approach is required, with the involvement of water companies, their customers, NRA and OFWAT. It will not be sufficient for water companies to merely address their distribution leakage levels or domestic metering without also taking action on customers' supply pipe leakage and adopting appropriate tariffs. The NRA does however recognise the possible social implications of domestic metering which need to be addressed by the government.

Opportunities also exist to achieve savings in the use of water by industry and agriculture. A good example is the Aire and Calder project where around 19% saving in water usage has been identified as a result of a systematic waste minimisation study involving eleven companies in Yorkshire. Not only does the reduced water use and other savings result in reduced environmental impact but also helps to reduce costs to the companies.

3.2.3
Future Resource Balance

Taking the three demand scenarios for each region in the year 2021 and comparing them with existing resources gives an indication of the potential scale of extra water resource developments that may be required in the next thirty years. Figure 5 shows the possible extent and magnitude of future imbalances if no additional water resources are developed. The data are derived from a consideration of resources and demands on a demand centre basis. A demand centre is a discrete area of demand in which given sources can supply the whole of that area and is more detailed than consideration of balances on a regional or company level.

The data assume that some reductions in yield are made to allow for reduced abstraction on environmental grounds. A total yield reduction of some 300 Ml/d has been allowed in the strategy to improve flows in low flow problem rivers and to account for reduced abstraction on environmental grounds from various over-stressed groundwater units. A degree of subjectivity has been adopted in arriving at this figure and the appropriate value will not be known until investigations are completed and value for money has been established. This loss of yield to water companies is assumed to be balanced by future development of acceptable replacement sources or reduced demand through improved leakage control or other demand management measures. In addition an 'outage' factor or contingency margin of 2.5% of total yields has been deducted to allow for the loss of yield caused by the possible operational failure of a source.

Figure 5 demonstrates that with demand management policies being employed at a limited level, as represented by the Medium scenario, the extent of future imbalances is reduced significantly when compared with the High scenario. In addition however, there will be 'local' developments which may offset some of the deficits shown in Figure 5. Appendix 1 shows the local resource development options which have been assumed to offset the deficits shown in Figure 5.

Adding these local options to the existing yield of the demand centres reduces the deficits at 2021 as shown in Figure 6. Any deficits remaining after the

Figure 5

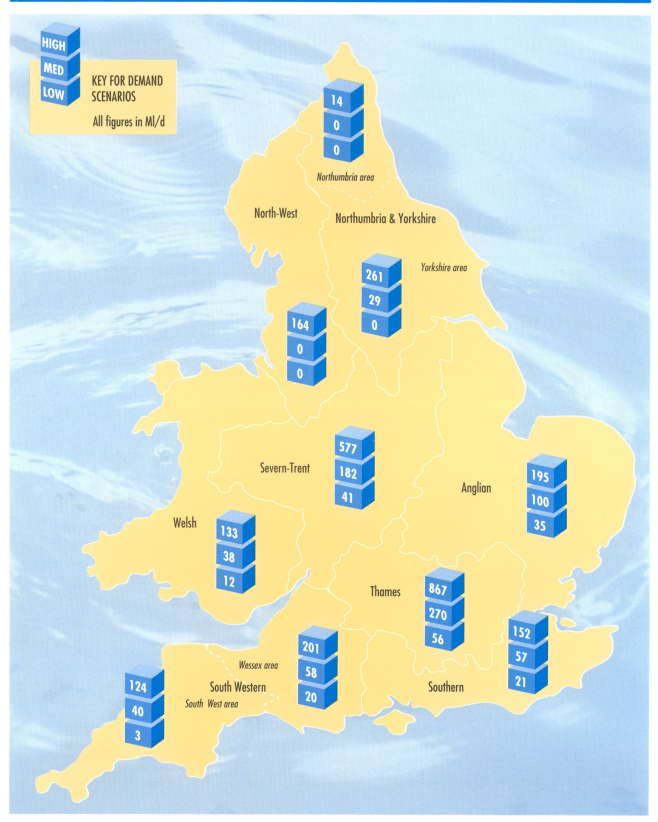

THE DO NOTHING DEFICITS
(SHORTFALL IN AVERAGE PUBLIC WATER SUPPLY YIELD IN 2021 WITH EXISTING SOURCE YIELDS UNDER A RANGE OF DEMAND SCENARIOS)

HIGH
MED
LOW

KEY FOR DEMAND SCENARIOS

All figures in Ml/d

14
0
0

Northumbria area

North-West

Northumbria & Yorkshire

261
29
0

Yorkshire area

164
0
0

577
182
41

Severn-Trent

195
100
35

Anglian

133
38
12

Welsh

867
270
56

Thames

152
57
21

Southern

201
58
20

Wessex area

South Western

South West area

124
40
3

These data are a summation of shortfalls at Demand Centre level.

development of local options shown in Figure 6 need to be satisfied by one or more strategic developments, and these arise only in the Anglian, Severn-Trent, Thames and Wessex regions.

It is important to stress that in Figures 5 and 6 the deficits shown are not those relating to a regionwide resource balance, but indicate that one or more demand centres within the region will be in deficit. In some instances the shortfall identified is accompanied by a surplus in other parts of the region, but such surpluses are often not transferable between demand centres.

3.2.4
Peak Demands

It is recognised that peak demands will have a bearing upon the balance between water resources and demand, especially in supply areas dependent upon groundwater sources. However for the purposes of preparing a broad national strategy, peaking has been taken to be a second order effect and has not been specifically considered. Clearly the development of detailed plans would require peak demand requirements to be taken into account.

3.3
INDUSTRIAL DEMANDS - DIRECT ABSTRACTION

Within the overall national water resources development strategy, it is important to consider demands arising from industrial users which abstract directly from rivers, estuaries or groundwater, as distinct from those supplied by public water supply companies described earlier. Direct abstraction of industrial demands account for 12% of the total volume of water abstracted. Industrial demand supplied by water companies is already accounted for within the demand forecasts for public water supply, but the direct abstraction of water needs to be considered separately.

The historic trend for directly abstracted industrial demand is shown in Figure 7. The trend in the last ten years or so has been a broadly declining demand. The reasons for this decline are varied, but significant effects can be attributed to a general fall in industrial production, plant closures and economic downturns. An increase in recycling and improvements in water use efficiency may also explain some of the decline.

In order to obtain an indication of the likely direction of future demand the Confederation of British Industry commissioned a demand survey for the NRA of industrial users across key sectors of the economy in England and Wales which included demands met from direct abstraction and public mains.

Of the companies surveyed almost two thirds (64%) indicated that demand for water in their sector would remain static or decrease in the planning period. Those who suggested a decrease estimated that it would be in the order of 10% or more. The main reasons given for this decline were similar to those stated above.

It appears that there is no specific requirement to plan for any overall increase in demand for direct abstraction for industry. Those industries predicting a small increase in demand will probably be offset by those predicting a decrease and therefore it seems reasonable to expect the current balance to remain for the foreseeable planning period.

Figure 6

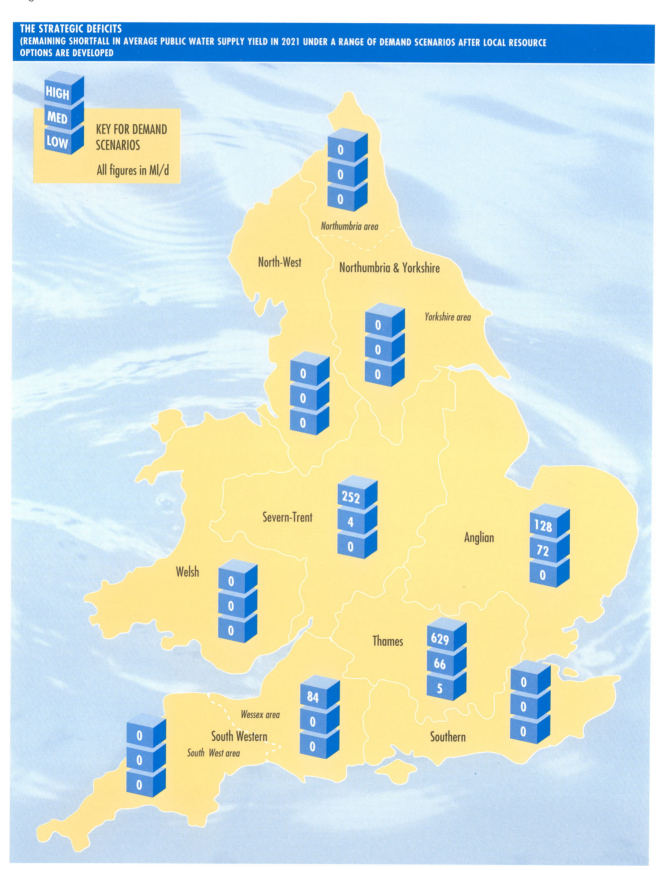

THE STRATEGIC DEFICITS
(REMAINING SHORTFALL IN AVERAGE PUBLIC WATER SUPPLY YIELD IN 2021 UNDER A RANGE OF DEMAND SCENARIOS AFTER LOCAL RESOURCE OPTIONS ARE DEVELOPED

HIGH
MED
LOW

KEY FOR DEMAND SCENARIOS

All figures in Ml/d

Northumbria area

North-West

Northumbria & Yorkshire

Yorkshire area

Severn-Trent

Anglian

Welsh

Thames

South Western

South West area

Wessex area

Southern

These data are a summation of shortfalls at Demand Centre level and represent the amount of demand in the region that would need to be met from strategic sources.

Figure 7

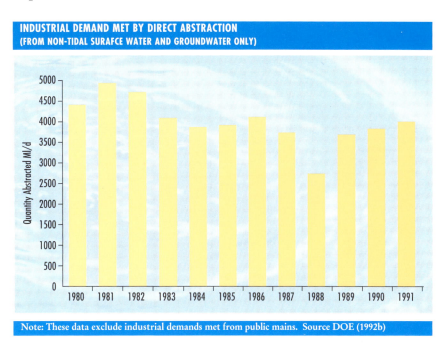

INDUSTRIAL DEMAND MET BY DIRECT ABSTRACTION
(FROM NON-TIDAL SURAFCE WATER AND GROUNDWATER ONLY)

Note: These data exclude industrial demands met from public mains. Source DOE (1992b)

An important consideration however is the future effect of incentive charging to manage the discharge of effluents. As tariffs increase, as may be expected, there will be increased incentives to use water more efficiently and this will reduce the demand for abstraction.

3.4

POWER GENERATION DEMANDS - DIRECT ABSTRACTION

Historically the demand for water from the power generation industry has remained relatively stable at about 36% of all abstraction excluding tidal water (see Figure 8). The large volumes of water required for through cooling, evaporative cooling and other purposes tend to be drawn from poor quality waters or waters which are tidal in nature. This water is usually returned to the river with little impact.

In order to assess the likely future demand for direct abstraction for power generation, the NRA invited all power companies currently operating in England and Wales to submit details of how and where they saw demand increasing in the next 30 years. Nearly 50% of companies responded and from an analysis of their comments there appears to be little reason to expect the trend in demand to change significantly over the planning period. Indeed, changes in technology and moves towards alternative methods of cooling seem likely to act in a way which will reduce gross demand.

Figure 8

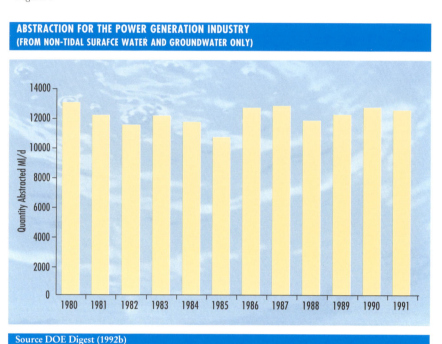

ABSTRACTION FOR THE POWER GENERATION INDUSTRY (FROM NON-TIDAL SURAFCE WATER AND GROUNDWATER ONLY)

Source DOE Digest (1992b)

3.5
AGRICULTURAL DEMAND

3.5.1
Present Demand and Resources

The agricultural demand for water is presently around 1% of the total water demand. In dry years most (over 70%) is used for spray irrigation, and is concentrated most heavily in the Anglian region. The remaining, non-irrigation agricultural demand, includes dairying, food processing and springs, wells and boreholes for domestic and general farm use. The non-irrigation demand for water is therefore relatively small and can normally be satisfied by local sources or mains supplies.

Spray irrigation on the other hand, has become of particular importance to ensure quality, reliability and continuity of produce at stable prices which are often essential marketing requirements. It is highly likely that in some sectors production would not take place unless a continuous water supply was available.

The demand for water for spray irrigation is also significant as it places high demands on groundwater, rivers and streams at times of the year when flows are at their lowest. Legislation (Section 57, Water Resources Act 1991) therefore gives the NRA special powers to restrict abstraction for spray irrigation during periods of exceptional shortage of rain, which the NRA uses to protect the environment from over-abstraction.

It is important to recognise that resources are not guaranteed since licences have often been granted by the NRA and its predecessors on the basis that abstraction will have to cease at flow rates specified in licences or when Section 57 restrictions are introduced in order to protect the environment. Alternatively licence applications could have been refused in such circumstances, but this would not have made best use of available water resources. This does however mean that the water resources are less reliable at a time when farmers need the water most.

During the recent drought, farmers were faced with limits on supplies of water through the effect of such licence conditions, naturally dry or low flow rivers or due to NRA restrictions imposed to protect the environment. Farmers who had already constructed sufficient on-farm storage did not face these difficulties, but elsewhere abstraction often needed to be cut back to avoid or reduce adverse environmental impact to wetlands and watercourses.

The peak drought demand for spray irrigation in some parts of the country is currently exceeding resource availability and the environment sometimes needs to be protected through the use of restrictions imposed by the NRA. These restrictions are never popular and ways need to be found to improve the efficient management and development of water for agriculture.

3.5.2
Future Demand

There has been little information published on the future agricultural use of water and a study was commissioned to forecast future requirements (Weatherhead *et al*, 1993). The best estimate of actual underlying growth in abstraction for irrigation over the 1982 - 1990 period, after allowing for weather differences between the census years, is around 2% per annum.

Future demand is expected to depend mainly on future agricultural policy, but also on technical and other factors. Changes in climate may also play a part, but have not been considered specifically in this strategy as predictions of change are not sufficiently firm at this stage.

Under the currently expected agricultural policy the 'most likely' forecast is that there will be a relatively minor increase in total irrigated area of 0.7% per annum from 1996 to 2001 and 0.3% per annum from 2001 to 2021. Growth in the total volume of water used will be greater but still modest, at 1.7% per annum from 1996 to 2001 and 1% per annum from 2001 to 2021. It is emphasised that these are demand forecasts and that actual usage may be constrained by restrictions on water availability, for whatever reason.

The increase in dry year irrigation water volumes for each NRA region is shown in Figure 9 which demonstrates the concentration of this demand in the Anglian and Severn-Trent regions which account for 75% of total demand.

Figure 9

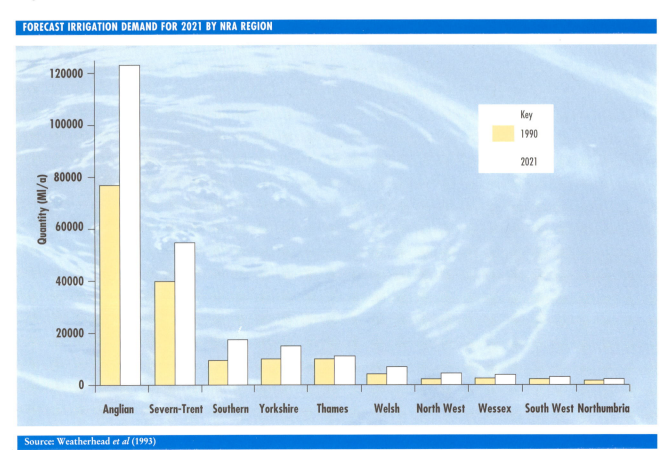

FORECAST IRRIGATION DEMAND FOR 2021 BY NRA REGION

Key
1990
2021

Source: Weatherhead *et al* (1993)

3.5.3
Options for
Meeting Demand

The options for meeting future demand will generally include the following:

● investment in new resources;

● management initiatives to re-allocate existing resources;

● improved efficiency in the use of resources.

The NRA has liaised with MAFF and other key organisations to provide a national focus for taking these issues forward. The following sections describe the possibilities in more detail.

3.5.4
Investment in
New Resources

In much of those regions where spray irrigation is most heavily concentrated, resources are already fully committed and there is little spare capacity to support further direct abstraction to meet future summer needs. Resources could however be made available by transferring water from sources with a surplus to areas of deficit or by storing spare winter water. This would however require substantial investment such as that which has been provided by other sectors to meet the needs of their processes or customers. In contrast with some sectors, there has been relatively little investment by the farming industry in medium to large scale resource development. The reasons for this are understood to include the following:

● the large cost of works for individual farmers relative to the return on the investment;

● the lack of a suitable organisation or institutional framework to promote collective needs and take a strategic view;

● the lack of available finance for large schemes and the short pay back periods demanded on loans;

● the lack of powers for farmers to construct works and to transfer water;

● the difficulty of meeting a distributed demand without a suitable infrastructure (assuming that it is not generally economic to use mains water for crops other than those of especially high value).

Despite these difficulties there have been various investment initiatives in recent years. The most common development option is for individual or small groups of irrigators to construct winter storage to support summer abstractions. In most parts of England and Wales winter water is still available for this type of storage, although the costs of construction vary depending on topography and ground conditions. Farmers often view construction as uneconomic, but it is possible to reduce unit costs by co-operative ventures which achieve economies of scale and management arrangements which allow a number of abstractors to benefit.

There are also examples of co-operation and investment by farmers which could form models for future investment. For instance, in the Anglian region:

● in the mid 1980s, 100 farmers provided £100k for transfer works, which allowed new licences to be granted from the receiving sources;

● in the early 1990s, 50 farmers formed a company to build and operate transfer works which also enabled the NRA to grant additional licences,

● 30 farmers in a fen area are considering pooling their licences into one licence held by an 'umbrella company' to allow greater flexibility and security, and hope to achieve economies of scale in the future construction of winter storage reservoirs.

Successful initiatives of this type need greater publicity to demonstrate the benefits available at relatively modest cost. They all involve a high degree of co-operation. Farmers have been willing to form co-operatives to market and in some cases process their products, but there has been little collaboration on water matters to date.

There are also various strategic options for increasing water availability in the Anglian region. For example:

● distribution of Trent water around the fens, by transfer via the rivers Witham and Ancholme;

● negotiating a share in possible water resources developments such as the Great Bradley or Fenland Reservoirs to spread additional resources throughout the South Level;

● exploring Section 20 Agreements for Rutland and/or Eyebrook reservoirs for similar schemes in the North and Middle Levels;

● substituting 'strategic' water for existing allocations to allow reallocation of local water to local needs.

The use of the Fen drainage system, and using substitution to release local water at the point of need may go some way to providing an 'infra-structure' to spread the benefit of additional water resources more widely.

The options for funding new developments are discussed more fully in Section 8, which describes the Finance, Promotion and Development of new schemes. The NRA considers that the exact balance between year to year farming practice and investment decisions to manage the risk of failure of supplies are matters for individual irrigators and the extent to which they are able to pass on the additional cost of resource development in the market place. Similarly, the Government itself no longer provides grants for winter storage, leaving farmers to decide for themselves the economics of investing in new sources of supply.

Although the NRA does not expect to finance new resource developments it will consider using its powers to construct works and transfer water subject to the funding being made available by third parties or the Government and the proposed development being environmentally acceptable. In addition the NRA has powers under Section 20 of the Water Resources Act 1991 to enter into agreements with water undertakers to make further resources available, but the NRA would expect the beneficiaries to meet the costs involved.

3.5.5
Management Initiatives

Arrangements for pooling and sharing water already allocated through licences could allow a more efficient distribution of resources. During the dry summer of 1990 for example, actual water utilisation in many catchments was only some 40% - 60% of the aggregated licensed quantity. The reasons for this situation are understood to include over-licensing due to changes in cropping, changes in business objectives and sales of farms. The co-operation of farmers in cutting back irrigation water usage at a time of drought may also explain some of the under-utilisation of licensed quantities.

There would therefore seem to be opportunities for farmers to collaborate over resource allocation with the aim of trying to preserve supplies for the whole of the season. Subject to compliance with statutory requirements and protection of the environment, arrangements could include:

● cash payments between farmers to 'buy out' water rights;

● pooling of licences by groups of farmers:

- within a new single licence, held perhaps by a co-operative, 'shareholders' could buy and sell water to suit their own needs for irrigation on the land holdings specified in the new licence. This could prove particularly effective in fen areas, on large lowland rivers or from deep/confined aquifers;

● under utilised boreholes or winter storage reservoirs could be used to augment rivers for abstraction downstream; or

● 'surplus' river flows could be used for irrigation early in the season and boreholes reserved for times when river flows are low:

- These schemes would be relatively simple for a single farmer to administer, but financial arrangements may be required when many farmers are involved;

● inter farm transfers:

- A farmer with surplus resources could vary his licence and pipe water to an adjacent farm with a deficit. Local geography rarely allows for this and the measures above are probably more appropriate.

The reallocation of licences through a system of tradeable permits could also improve the economic efficiency of allocating abstraction rights. In addition spray irrigation demand could be controlled by a system of incentive charges. These approaches would require a change in the legislation and controls to ensure the protection of the environment.

3.5.6
Improved Efficiency

Improvements in the efficiency of irrigation might also make better use of available resources, through the development of improved irrigation techniques in terms of time of application, improvements in operating practices and the development of better operating systems. There seems to be some evidence however, that more scientific scheduling of irrigation water could result in increased water usage as most scheduling systems are aimed at maximising crop production, rather than at water economy.

4. DEVELOPMENT OPTIONS

4.1
INTRODUCTION

The resource development options proposed to meet possible deficits can be considered to be either 'local options', often close to the area of demand, or 'strategic options' which are generally larger schemes, sometimes remote from the area of need, as has been referred to earlier. It is assumed in this strategy that 'local options' would be developed first to meet incremental demand and that strategic resource developments would be considered as options for meeting those deficits which are forecast to remain after current and local developments have been taken into account.

4.2
LOCAL OPTIONS

The inclusion of a scheme as a local option does not necessarily imply that its promotion would be acceptable to the NRA, since full environmental impact assessments will be needed before acceptance. Nor should the quoted yield be taken as a firm estimate. A schedule of the local options assumed in this strategy is given in Appendix 1.

It is noted that the magnitude of the total yield of the local options is significant (some 2051 Ml/d). Although the national strategy does not attempt to analyse the local options it is clear that where development is likely to be required it will be necessary to bring each local scheme up to a common degree of confidence in terms of environmental acceptability and available yield for supply. At present the local options comprise a mixture of schemes of different types and degrees of investigation. Although groundwater development does not feature strongly as a strategic option (see Section 4.3 below), many of the local options rely on the development of groundwaters which are normally good quality sources, close to the point of use and can be constructed in stages to match the pace of demand. However, in broad terms, the potential for further large scale groundwater development is extremely limited in England and Wales.

Although it has been assumed that local options will be constructed first, strategic development in some circumstances may be a better alternative to a number of small local developments. This is a matter to be addressed in the future.

4.3
STRATEGIC OPTIONS

The NRA in consultation with water supply companies has identified a number of strategic resource options for investigation as components of the national water resources strategy. The identified strategic options relate both to sources of additional water and schemes for the distribution of water.

Options identified as key components for consideration in the national strategy are listed below and are shown in Figure 10:

● River Severn to River Thames Transfer;

● Enlarged Craig Goch Reservoir;

Figure 10

STRATEGIC OPTIONS CONSIDERED IN THE STRATEGY

- Redeployed Vyrnwy Reservoir;

- South West Oxfordshire Reservoir;

- River Severn to River Trent Transfer;

- Canal transfer to the River Thames;

- East Anglian Reservoir;

- River Trent to East Anglia Transfer;

- Birmingham Rising Groundwater.

Although the yield of Birmingham rising groundwater is small relative to the other strategic options it does nevertheless offer the potential to serve several centres of demand, including use as a source for transfer via canal. For these reasons the option has been considered as strategic.

These options are considered both in the financial and environmental analysis. Each of the options is described in Appendix 2 both in terms of configuration, capital costs, capacities, yields and environmental issues. The strategy is then formulated in Chapters 6 and 7 taking account of the range of relevant factors.

Kielder reservoir in the north-east of England was originally considered to be a strategic option, since up to 500Ml/d of spare yield could be available for use outside the region. The reservoir was completed in 1982 and was expected to be used to meet the predicted industrial and public water supply deficiencies in Newcastle and Teeside which did not materialise.

A study into the cost of transferring this water to the south east indicates that Kielder is unlikely to be an economic alternative to the other strategic schemes which have been identified. It remains a possibility however that Kielder could be useful in meeting marginal deficits in parts of Yorkshire.

4.4
TIMESCALES REQUIRED TO IMPLEMENT MAJOR OPTIONS

Recent experience has shown that it can take between 15 and 25 years to investigate, promote and construct a major new water resource in the UK. Figure 11 shows the implementation programmes for five recent schemes. The factors tending to prolong the programmes are:

- increasing concern over environmental issues and pressure from land owners and nature conservation bodies;

- difficulties over proving the need for the scheme;

- disputes over the ultimate size of the scheme;

- the need to investigate several schemes in detail, before deciding on the preferred option.

These factors have led to protracted public inquiries and, in several cases, more than one public inquiry for a particular option.

A feature of this is that these factors are difficult to predict. There are also uncertainties in the possibility of some schemes needing to be promoted by more than one water company. Although in theory it is possible to investigate, promote, construct and fill a major new reservoir in, say 10 to 12 years, it would be prudent to allow at least 20 years for this process.

Figure 11

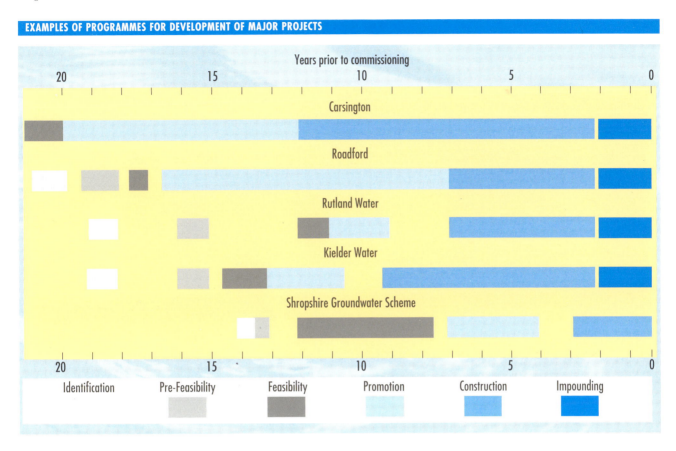

EXAMPLES OF PROGRAMMES FOR DEVELOPMENT OF MAJOR PROJECTS

Years prior to commissioning

Carsington

Roadford

Rutland Water

Kielder Water

Shropshire Groundwater Scheme

Identification   Pre-Feasibility   Feasibility   Promotion   Construction   Impounding

4.5
OPTIONS EXCLUDED

4.5.1

Barrages

There are many environmental uncertainties about the construction of a tidal barrage which fully encloses and floods an estuary. In addition, where the tidal flow is large it may not be technically feasible.

The construction of smaller, bunded reservoirs, occupying only a part of an estuary, may be achieved without significant environmental implications, depending upon the proposed size of the reservoir and sensitivity of the location. Due to the nature of the environment, the cost of reservoir construction could be higher in an estuary than inland. There would therefore be little advantage in an estuary reservoir, unless its scale makes it preferable to inland development.

Bunded reservoirs on the Wash Estuary have previously been considered to meet demands in East Anglia and are estimated to yield up to 450 Ml/d. However, their costs are likely to be greater than conventional alternatives and the environmental disbenefits larger. Similar estuary storages in Morecambe Bay are too remote from the centres of demand to be an important strategic source.

A barrage on the River Dee would provide an alternative source in the North West but it is unlikely that the development of a full barrage or pumped storage reservoir could be successfully promoted due to the environmental sensitivity of the area.

It has been concluded that from a water resources viewpoint no future investigation work on tidal barrages is justified in the foreseeable future.

4.5.2
Artificial Recharge of Groundwater

Artificial recharge is a technique for supplementing the natural infiltration to an aquifer using surplus water for use at times of drought. To be cost-effective, there must be a reasonably convenient source of recharge water of suitable quality and natural hydrogeological conditions which ensure that sufficient water is retained within the aquifer for use when it is needed.

Such conditions are rare in the UK, although parts of the London Basin are a good example. The usefulness of recharge is already demonstrated in this area by schemes in the Lee Valley and at Enfield-Haringey. Opportunities in South London are also being studied. Elsewhere, only the Sherwood sandstones of the Cheshire Basin have the appropriate structure on a similar scale; however more localised opportunities may exist, associated for example, with geological folds.

Estimates of cost suggest that artificial recharge could represent a relatively cheap option, which has limited environmental impact. It is therefore considered that further study is needed to identify areas with geological conditions which are potentially favourable before any groundwater recharge schemes are included as potential strategic options.

4.5.3
Effluent Re-use

The potential resource available from direct and indirect re-use schemes is considerable. Effluent re-use appears from the few studies carried out, to be a relatively cheap option which can be developed without significant environmental impact. However, progress towards establishment of direct re-use as a standard source of potable water is likely to be cautious and slow because of public health concerns.

The resource advantages of indirect re-use as practised in the Thames Basin, for example, are well established, and it is considered that other similar opportunities should be actively evaluated.

Studies have been carried out within the Thames Water Utilities and Essex Water Company areas to examine effluent re-use in the London area. Successful promotion of such schemes and their acceptance by customers are seen as critical tests before a more general widening of re-use practice can begin. This strategy has however assumed that a re-use scheme for the London area can be developed as a source of water for potable use at a rate of 30 Ml/d.

4.5.4
Desalination

In general, desalination is too expensive to be considered as an important water resource option in the UK. There are methods by which the cost of desalination can be reduced substantially - such as combined desalination and power generation facilities and treatment of saline groundwater. However, these opportunities are very localised and in general they could not be linked easily to a national strategy.

It is recognised that in certain specific situations, such as to meet peak summer demands in tourist areas like the Channel Islands, desalination can provide an economically viable water resource. However, it is considered that desalination is not appropriate for inclusion as a strategic option within the national water resources strategy.

4.5.5
Undersea Pipelines

The cost per unit length of laying an undersea pipeline can be twice that of an equivalent land pipeline. However, construction and operation of offshore pipelines is a well developed technology, largely due to experience within the oil industry. Should the need for water exceed the High demand scenario, an offshore pipeline transfer of water from the wetter North to the drier South and East of England would warrant further consideration. It would also have the advantage that it could be implemented in a relatively short time due to the reduced planning and perceived environmental implications.

4.5.6
Flexible Tankers and Flexible Water Sacs

Shipment of bulk transfers by tanker are considered to be too expensive but the towing of water filled bags is being given serious consideration within the private sector. This novel idea would require a seaward terminal at the filling and supply end of the route. Bags containing tens of thousands of tonnes of water are thought to be feasible and it is possible that the unit costs of water delivered could be reasonably competitive. However, until such time as the technology is proven and the operational risks are acceptable to users it is considered prudent not to include this option as an alternative within the strategy.

4.5.7
Future Work

Whilst the above options have not been included as specific options in the development of the strategy, further work may show them to be more acceptable and/or competitive. If this is the case, they may well impact upon the strategy in due course.

5. ENVIRONMENTAL ASSESSMENTS

5.1
GENERAL PRINCIPLES

In order to ensure the proper use of water resources the NRA supports the principle of sustainable development. This requires that surface and groundwater resources are not diminished by excessive abstraction or pollution and that resource development does not erode the natural assets supported by rivers and the aquatic environment.

Taken in its widest context, sustainable development includes social, economic and environmental issues which will need to be addressed primarily by the government, the NRA and OFWAT. Policies for sustainable development will need to be developed by these organisations taking into account advice from the many groups and individuals who can make a valuable contribution.

To minimise disruption to the water environment, the most appropriate option for meeting water resources needs in the long term is to reduce leakage and to introduce other demand management measures so that as few schemes are developed as necessary. The reallocation of spare resources already developed can also help to limit the need for new schemes. It is also important that the quality of existing resources is protected from pollution and that planned improvements are made where necessary to secure future supplies. Statutory Water Quality Objectives and the NRA's Groundwater Protection Policy (NRA, 1992b) will be of particular importance in this respect.

Where it can be shown that new resources need to be developed, the impact of different options on water quality, fisheries and the aquatic and terrestrial ecology will all need to be assessed in detail before conclusions can be drawn about the most appropriate option. Monitoring the environment and predictive modelling of the impacts of proposed schemes will be an essential part of the decision making process. This must be carried out carefully using the best methods available as it is in everyone's long term interests to conserve and improve the environment, on which human life and economic development depend. Even then there may still be uncertainties and a precautionary approach will be required where the risks to the environment are unacceptable. Priority attention must be given to sites of national and international importance (SPA, RAMSAR, SSSIs) and it will also be essential to compare the impact of local development options with those of the strategic developments, to ensure that the minimum environmental impact results from the overall strategy.

Environmental Assessments can take many years to complete and it is therefore important that preferred options are identified at an early stage to allow a satisfactory period for investigation and consultation.

5.2

The NRA has received considerable support for its approach to catchment management planning and it is essential that the strategy for water resources development is integrated into future catchment management plans prepared in consultation with interested bodies and the public. This will enable the NRA and others to take individual catchment needs into account, balancing these with the national objectives to protect sites of high conservation value and to rehabilitate those which have been degraded. The objective should be to make open decisions which best meet the needs of the community and the environment.

As further policies are developed on the application of minimum acceptable flows in response to research into environmentally acceptable flow regimes, catchment management plans will be used to implement national policies taking local circumstances and concerns into account.

The catchment management planning process is also intended to be used for implementing Statutory Water Quality Objectives. These objectives will represent a strategic approach to setting targets for the future quality of particular stretches of river and will need to be taken into account when planning future resource developments.

5.3

**ENVIRONMENTAL ASSESSMENT
OF STRATEGIC OPTIONS**

A preliminary environmental assessment has been completed to identify the environmental implications for each of the strategic options considered in Section 4.3. The purpose of the assessment is to highlight the key environmental issues which may favour or discriminate against particular options.

This assessment has involved an evaluation of the options based on:

● studies of individual schemes which have already been undertaken;

● a review of the impacts of existing UK schemes to identify the lessons to be learnt for future schemes;

● a literature review of the environmental issues and known impacts associated with water resources development schemes, including the effects of river regulation, inter-basin transfer and changes to residual flows to estuaries;

● an assessment of the environmental implications of the options taking account of the results of hydrological modelling of specific schemes.

An overview of the preliminary environmental assessment of strategic options is given in Appendix 3 which presents a broad view of the sensitivity of the natural environment associated with each option, the risk of change to the environment due to the operation of a new scheme and the overall potential impact of a development taking these two key factors into account. There are also benefit opportunities from new developments which are highlighted in the assessment. It is too early to draw firm conclusions about preferred options since more detailed studies need to be carried out. It may also be possible to build in further benefits which may not have been identified at this early stage and which may counter balance some of the environmental changes. A brief summary of the key environmental issues associated with each option is described in the following sections. Further details of each option are presented in Appendix 2.

5.4
SUMMARY OF
ENVIRONMENTAL EFFECTS

5.4.1
River Severn-
River Thames Transfer

Transfer of water from the River Severn to the River Thames could have adverse effects on its water quality and aquatic biology. Water would be abstracted from the lowland reaches of the River Severn, with contributions from upland limestone catchments, groundwater from drift and Triassic sandstone, and sewage and industrial effluent from urban conurbations. The discharge would be into the upland part of the River Thames catchment which is dominated by groundwater flow at times when flows in the River Thames would be naturally low. Detailed environmental assessment is needed to determine the significance of such potential impacts. However, in terms of water quality, there is a real risk of causing a significant change to the chemistry of the upper Thames despite the superficial similarity of NWC class between the lower Severn and upper Thames.

The potential impact of a River Severn to River Thames transfer on the River Severn itself can be mitigated by the adoption of a suitable prescribed flow and other abstraction rules. With these provisions, the impact on the River Severn system would not be expected to be significant. Equally, the terrestrial impacts of construction of the pipeline from the River Severn to the River Thames can be mitigated and there are potential benefits by rehabilitating part of the old Severn to Thames canal for some of the water transfer route.

5.4.2
Enlarged Craig Goch

The enlargement of the Craig Goch reservoir in the upper reaches of the River Wye catchment would provide a potentially large storage through the construction of a new dam on the site of an existing dam built as part of the original Elan Valley scheme.

Although the valley is one which has already been subject to much alteration through the original Victorian scheme, there is a potential for highly significant impact on the important Elenydd SSSI. However, the magnitude of the impact would depend to some extent on the size of reservoir constructed. On the other hand, the impact of the enlarged Craig Goch reservoir on agriculture and local population would be slight when compared with lowland reservoir schemes such as the South West Oxfordshire reservoir or Great Bradley.

The Craig Goch scheme could be used to supply the deficits in south east England through regulation of either the River Wye or the River Severn. The River Wye is highly sensitive environmentally, being a SSSI of national significance throughout its length as well as a famous salmon river. Further regulation of river flows could have potentially serious impacts. However there might also be some benefit through increased flows during the summer months. Use of Craig Goch to regulate the River Severn would have potentially much less significant impacts, because the River Severn's hydrological system is already substantially altered by schemes such as Clywedog reservoir and the Shropshire groundwater development. The impacts on the Severn system would however need to be carefully evaluated to ensure that significant environmental thresholds were not breached, but it seems probable that an acceptable scheme could be found, possibly by restricting the ultimate size of the Craig Goch scheme. The use of Craig Goch to regulate the Severn would still leave some impact on high flows in the River Wye which would need to be assessed.

5.4.3
Redeployed Vyrnwy Reservoir

Regulation of River Severn flows to feed the River Severn to River Thames transfer could also be provided through partial redeployment of Vyrnwy reservoir. The main impact of the scheme would be on the flows within the River Vyrnwy sub-catchment. The key issue would be the effect on salmonid nursery areas due to substantial increases in low flows during the summer which could wash out the salmon and trout fry.

These impacts would need to be carefully investigated. There would also be potential impact due to the release of low level water from Vyrnwy reservoir, although this could be avoided by the construction of a new multi-level reservoir draw-off facility.

5.4.4
South West Oxfordshire Reservoir

The construction of the South West Oxfordshire reservoir near Abingdon would create a major new storage at a strategic location within the Thames catchment. About 14 square kilometres (3,500 acres) of land would need to be utilised.

However, as the land is mainly classified as Grade 3 for agricultural use, the loss would not be particularly significant either in agricultural terms or with regard to effects on sites of nature conservation interest, which are few in the area. The construction of embankments up to 25 metres high would have a significant visual impact in an area which is substantially overlooked by high ground. However, the presence of Didcot power station in the vicinity has already reduced the visual amenity value of the area, so the reservoir would need to be seen in that context.

The construction of the reservoir would also create substantial short-term disturbance to the local population and there would be other construction impacts such as noise, increased traffic and pollution of water courses due to construction activities which could only partially be mitigated. On the other hand, there would be long-term benefits to the area in terms of recreational potential and amenity value. The operation of the South West Oxfordshire reservoir would have impacts on the fisheries and aquatic biology of the River Thames system which need further detailed investigation. However, the reservoir would offer the potential for storage of water if transferred from the River Severn and would help mitigate potential impacts of transferring River Severn water into the Thames.

5.4.5

River Severn to River Trent Transfer

Transferring water from the River Severn to the River Trent, ultimately to supply the East Midlands and possibly East Anglia, is expected to have comparatively low environmental impact upon the River Trent. There would be some effects of regulation on the Rivers Penk and Sow. However, the rivers are at present of low water quality, so the addition of better quality water from the River Severn would probably lead to an overall improvement. There would be some risk of transfer of fish diseases which needs further investigation.

The impact of the transfer on the River Severn system can be mitigated by choice of an appropriate prescribed flow and other operating rules. Construction impact of the pipelines can also be mitigated through careful route selection and design.

5.4.6

Canal Transfers

The use of the British Waterways canal system to transfer water from the Severn or Trent systems to the River Thames could have adverse effects on the Thames system. The particular concern would be the discharge of poor quality, often eutrophic, canal water into the Thames with the consequent potential for algal growth in the river. The carrying capacity of the canals would need to be increased by dredging and work on the banks, which would affect the nature conservation interests of the canals, including a number of SSSIs.

However, bearing in mind that the canals are themselves a man-made system, such impacts can be considered to be short-term and potentially mitigable. The impacts on the canal system would need to be studied in detail and would depend to some extent on the amount of water to be transferred. Any impacts would be offset by the potential for more assured supplies of water to the canal system during the summer and possible associated amenity improvements.

5.4.7

East Anglian Reservoir

Should a reservoir be constructed in East Anglia the main options appear to be at Great Bradley or a Fenland site. The impact of the Great Bradley reservoir would be very dependent upon the size of scheme eventually selected. At its largest potential size, the reservoir would have severe impacts on a SSSI and other sites of nature conservation interest, as well as the local population and farming community. However, the impacts would be substantially reduced if a smaller scheme was selected. In any event, a full environmental assessment would be undertaken before a decision on scheme size and promotion could be reached.

An alternative reservoir site on the Fenlands has not yet been investigated in detail, but could provide a reservoir of comparable size to Great Bradley, but with less environmental impact (but probably higher cost).

The operation of the East Anglian reservoir, regardless of the choice of sites, would have potentially significant impacts on the Ely-Ouse system and on the Wash. There would also be potential regulation effects on the Rivers Stour and Blackwater which may see an improvement in water quality and in-stream ecology during periods of low flows.

5.4.8
River Trent to
East Anglia Transfer

A further development to meet demand in East Anglia involves the transfer of surplus water from the Lower Trent to the existing Ely Ouse-Essex transfer system and onwards towards Essex. The main environmental concern with this option relates to water quality effects in the Rivers Stour and Blackwater which would need to be investigated in more detail.

5.4.9
Birmingham
Rising Groundwater

The water table below the Birmingham area is rising due to the decline in industrial abstraction making resources available to augment the River Trent or the canal system.

The water quality of these sources may improve by the addition of groundwater. The control of the water table by carefully managed abstraction could also prevent water levels rising into contaminated land and polluting other sources.

5.4.10
General Considerations

For a number of the strategic options, the potential environmental impact will be dependent upon the size of scheme selected. This applies particularly to the Craig Goch reservoir, regulation of the River Severn (or Wye), and the East Anglian reservoir. The size of scheme selected will be dependent upon the demand ultimately to be met and whether the demand can partially be met by other schemes. Therefore, the impact of individual schemes cannot be taken in isolation and due regard in the planning process will need to be taken of the comparative impacts of other competing schemes.

5.5
KEY ISSUES

Some of the key issues arising from the preliminary assessment relate to:

- the effect on flora and fauna of mixing water of different chemistries;

- the transfer of species and diseases between catchments;

- the loss of terrestrial habitats due to reservoir construction;

- the effect of changed river flow regimes on fish movement;

- the possible benefits which can be obtained from specific options.

Of particular concern to the NRA, are the inherent risks in transferring large quantities of water into adjacent catchments, which relate to biological integrity, transfer of pathogens and diseases, predatory species and 'finger printing' confusion for migrating salmonids. Particular risks are associated with transfers from the downstream end of large lowland rivers into the headwaters of upland or middle order reaches, due to the disruption of the nutrient cycle. The presence of existing connections between catchments through the existing canal network does however negate some of the arguments concerning biological integrity.

From an examination of existing schemes, such as the regulated River Wye which is a designated SSSI, there does not appear to be a fundamental reason why such water resources schemes cannot be built and operated without causing severe environmental deterioration. However, this will require careful scheme design and selection based upon detailed environmental impact assessment and where possible, cost benefit analysis taking account of environmental and engineering costs.

5.6
CONCLUSION/SUMMARY

The high level environmental assessment has identified the key issues associated with each of the options based on assumptions about reservoir size and rates of regulation releases and transfers. The approach adopted has generally been to consider the 'worst case' and there may be variants of the assessed options which have significantly less impacts or important benefits.

It is an inescapable fact however that all reservoir construction and inter-basin transfers will have some impact on the aquatic environment. A policy of 'no change' is unrealistic, and would mean that no development could be supported. The central issue for the NRA is to question the need for the development and the scale and significance of any environmental change which may occur. It is clear that further option specific studies will need to be undertaken to improve the understanding of the environmental implications and baseline conditions for the more promotable options. Only when these detailed assessments are complete will it be possible for the NRA to consider a licence application for a new scheme.

6. FINANCIAL COST ANALYSIS

6.1
INTRODUCTION

The formulation of a long term strategy for water resources development needs to account for uncertainties in future demand, risks and benefits to the environment, risk to abstractors, and the overall financial and economic costs.

This report concentrates on the financial costs rather than economic costs since there is a current lack of adequate economic cost and benefit estimates of potential environmental impacts given the complexity of the development options investigated. Appendix 4 lists the Research and Development projects that the NRA is sponsoring with a view to estimating the costs and benefits of a variety of water environment inputs. In time it will become possible to appraise the environmental impacts of a range of schemes in economic terms.

The strategy formulation has adopted a 'UK Limited' perspective and no account has been taken of political, national or financial aspirations of individual organisations. A financial analysis has been used to see which development options would be chosen if engineering and operating costs were the only determining factors. Further analyses have been carried out to examine whether variations in basic assumptions would alter the findings. Such analyses have included the total removal of one or more development options from consideration as well as the variation of the details of individual schemes. The results of the financial cost analysis have subsequently been taken into account alongside environmental and other implications in the formulation of the strategy.

6.2
ANALYSIS

A computerised water resources planning model has been used to select the least net present cost (NPC) strategy over the planning period to the year 2021 for a given set of options and future demand scenarios. The NPC is the total discounted capital and pumping cost over the period using the Treasury discount rate of 6% per annum. Operating costs were based on pumping costs on the basis that other operating costs are likely to be similar and hence can be excluded from the analysis. The implication is that transfer schemes will normally have higher operating costs than reservoirs due to the amount of pumping usually required. Because the analysis considers only the demands which cannot be met from existing and 'local' schemes, the results of the analysis represent only the marginal costs of developing resources to meet the marginal demand. No attempt has been made to evaluate costs of meeting the total demand. Additionally, where a scheme component is common to all possible strategies, this has not been costed.

6.3
TREATMENT OF
DEMAND SCENARIOS

The NRA does not consider that a long term strategy should be based upon a specific prediction of a particular future demand, but instead it should be recognised that forecasting is an uncertain process. This is especially so at present, due not only to lack of knowledge of future economic activity, but also doubts regarding the long term impacts of demand management initiatives.

The approach has been to examine the need for resource development for each of the Low, Medium and High demand scenarios in turn. Initial analyses were carried out to select the schemes which gave the lowest net present cost of development over the planning period. However in recognition that cost is just one of several considerations in striving for an environmentally efficient strategy, alternative development options were also analysed from a range of other viewpoints.

The primary considerations leading to the preparation of an appropriate strategy are:

- environmental impacts;

- opportunities for flexible development;

- durations for development;

- operational risks;

- degrees of acceptability to water companies.

All these factors need to be taken into account in the formulation of the strategy by using a multi-criteria analysis as well as examining engineering costs and demand uncertainty.

6.4
MEETING THE LOW DEMAND SCENARIO

With the Low demand scenario there are generally sufficient local schemes available to meet any demand requirements and hence no strategic resource development would be necessary.

6.5
MEETING THE MEDIUM DEMAND SCENARIO

6.5.1
Results of the Financial Analysis

To meet demands in accordance with the Medium demand scenario only three strategic developments are required.

The first development would be needed within the period 2006 to 2011 to meet a marginal demand arising in the Anglian region. This would involve the construction of an East Anglian reservoir. Between 2011 and 2016 a transfer from the River Severn would be needed to meet demands arising in the Thames catchment, and between 2016 and 2021 the development of Birmingham Rising Groundwater would be required.

The sequence of scheme development is summarised below:

Scheme	To Meet Marginal Demands in:	Approximate Period Needed
East Anglian Reservoir	Anglian Region	2006-2011
Unsupported River Severn to River Thames Transfer	Thames Region	2011-2016
Birmingham Rising Groundwater	East Midlands	2016-2021

If it is not feasible to develop a reservoir in East Anglia then the next cheapest alternative would be the construction of a transfer from the River Trent to link with the existing Ely Ouse-Essex transfer scheme.

If it is not feasible to develop a transfer from the River Severn to the River Thames then the option would be either to:

● construct a South West Oxfordshire reservoir; or

● provide a fully piped transfer from the River Severn to the London area.

Analysis indicates that for the Medium demand scenario the net present cost would be some £57M cheaper to construct the piped transfer to the London area rather than developing South West Oxfordshire reservoir.

6.5.2

Summary of Costs of Meeting the Medium Demand Scenario

Total capital and net present costs are given below for each of the alternatives considered above.

Schemes	Total Capital Costs £M	Net Present Costs £M
East Anglian Reservoir (2006-2011) River Severn to River Thames Transfer (2011-2016) Birmingham Rising Groundwater (2016-2021)	273	63
East Anglian Reservoir (2006-2011) Piped Transfer from River Severn to London Birmingham Rising Groundwater (2016-2021)	333	72
East Anglian Reservoir (2006-2011) South West Oxfordshire Reservoir (2011-2016) Birmingham Rising Groundwater (2016-2021)	581	129

6.6
MEETING THE
HIGH DEMAND SCENARIO

6.6.1
Results of the
Financial Analysis

A base case analysis was carried out to identify the least overall discounted costs of meeting the High demand scenario over the planning period and resulted in the following sequence of scheme development:

Scheme	To Meet Marginal Demands in:-	Approx. Period Needed
Unsupported River Severn to River Thames Transfer	Thames region	By 1996
Partial Vyrnwy Redeployment	W. Midlands, Wessex & Thames regions	2001-2006
East Anglian Reservoir	Anglian region	2001-2006
Enlarged Craig Goch	W. Midlands, Wessex & Thames regions	2006-2011
River Severn to River Trent Transfer	East Midlands	2011-2016
South West Oxfordshire Reservoir	Thames region	2016-2021
Birmingham Rising Groundwater	East Midlands	2006-2011

The total capital cost associated with the above schemes is some £880M and the net present costs amount to £353M.

Clearly from the indicative timing for such schemes a number would be unable to be developed in time. In particular the River Severn to Thames transfer could not be in place by the mid 1990s and one would doubt whether the East Anglian reservoir or Craig Goch could be implemented in time.

6.6.2
Alternative Options

Because different schemes have different environmental and other implications, further 'what if' examinations have been carried out on alternative options so that the resulting strategy can be based on as wide a range of considerations as possible. A number of questions have been posed:

i)
What if the River Severn
to River Thames transfer
is unacceptable?

If the River Severn to River Thames transfer is unacceptable for environmental or other reasons, theoretically a South West Oxfordshire reservoir would be needed in the mid 1990's under the High demand scenario. Clearly this is not possible. A South West Oxfordshire reservoir would then become fully committed between 2006 and 2011, by which time a further source would be required.

If the direct transfer from the River Severn to the River Thames is unacceptable, it is possible that a direct transfer from the River Severn to a South West Oxfordshire reservoir would be more acceptable. If this is so then a River Severn to South West Oxfordshire reservoir transfer would need to be in place during the period 2006 to 2011 and would be further supported from an enlarged Craig Goch reservoir sometime between 2011 and 2016.

Total capital costs for this alternative are essentially the same as the base case although the net present costs rise by some £284M. In the event that no River Severn water could be allowed to enter the River Thames, then a possible alternative could be a direct pipeline from the River Severn to the London area. Further work would be required to be satisfied that the chemical effects on water mains would be acceptable. The sequence and timing of development would be similar to the base case for the High demand scenario. The total capital costs would rise to some £1,000M and the net present costs would amount to £457M. Although the direct pipeline to London gives total net present costs which are around £104M more than the base case, this option is still about £180M less costly than constructing a South West Oxfordshire reservoir first.

ii)

What would be the effect of utilising effluent re-use in the London area?

The possible re-use of treated sewage effluent in the London area is being investigated by Thames Water Utilities. Although there are examples of direct re-use of sewage effluents in other countries there are, at present, doubts regarding public health risks and acceptability of such methods to the general public.

However, as an example of the possible strategic implications of practising direct re-use, financial analysis has been carried out assuming that a 100 Ml/d source would be available for the London area. The effect is to delay the possible need for the River Severn to River Thames transfer from the mid 1990's to between the years 2006 to 2011 and to delay the need for South West Oxfordshire reservoir beyond the planning horizon. Total capital costs of meeting the High demand scenario, assuming that such re-use would be introduced in the mid 1990s is £517M. Total net present costs amount to about £330M which is the lowest of all the High demand scenario alternatives.

iii)

Is there an alternative to constructing a reservoir in East Anglia?

In financial terms, the next cheapest option to the construction of a reservoir in East Anglia is to transfer unsupported River Trent water to the Ely Ouse and onwards to the Essex region via the existing Ely Ouse-Essex transfer scheme. Reservoir costs have been based upon those available for the Great Bradley site, but investigation of another site on the Fens is underway by Essex Water Company.

As in the base case for the High demand scenario a new supply is required in East Anglia sometime between 1996 and 2006 and the replacement of a reservoir option with a River Trent transfer option results in the net present costs of meeting the marginal demands for the High demand scenario being £45M higher than the base case. When further information becomes available on the feasibility of an alternative reservoir on the Fens it will be necessary to carry out a more detailed and exhaustive analysis in order to determine the relative merits of reservoir and transfer alternatives on financial, economic and environmental grounds.

6.7

SUMMARY OF FINANCIAL ANALYSIS

The analyses have been directed at examining which schemes would be chosen to meet the Low, Medium or High demand scenario, if the least overall cost of engineering works and pumping were the determining criteria. For the Low scenario no strategic schemes are required. For the High scenario the total capital cost of the base case schemes required over the planning period approaches £900M and involves three significant reservoir schemes with the East Anglian reservoir required first, followed by enlargement of Craig Goch reservoir and finally the South West Oxfordshire reservoir near the end of the planning period.

In addition, a River Severn to River Thames transfer would be required early in the planning period and subsequently backed up by partial redeployment from Vyrnwy reservoir and eventually the enlargement of Craig Goch reservoir. A River Severn to River Trent transfer would also be needed near the end of the planning period.

Alternatives are presented for the High scenario if certain key components are removed or added. With modest demand management achievements it is likely that future demands will be similar to the Medium scenario or lower. This Medium demand scenario results in a relatively small requirement for strategic water resources development based upon a reservoir in East Anglia within the next 15 to 20 years and either a River Severn to Thames transfer or the South West Oxfordshire reservoir in about 20 years time.

The potential developments for the Medium demand scenario are seen as a subset of those required for the High demand scenario. In broad terms the schedule of scheme developments for the High demand scenario can be viewed as a possible sequence of future scheme development (when based solely on an engineering and operating cost basis) but with the dates of implementation depending upon the actual demand which arises.

As has already been pointed out, a strategy cannot be developed purely from consideration of engineering costs and many other factors need to be taken into account in its formulation. These have inlcuded:

● environmental implications;

● flexibility and timescale for implementation;

● uncertainty regarding future demands;

● operational security.

7. STRATEGY CONCLUSIONS

GENERAL CONCLUSIONS

● There is a marked contrast between the scale of water resource development needed to meet the Low, Medium and High demand scenarios. It is the NRA's view that there is a good chance that demand can be managed to generally achieve future demand levels close to or even substantially below the Medium scenario, meaning that there is a real possibility that no strategic resources will need to be completed in England and Wales for perhaps 20 years or more.

● The current attention being given to demand management opportunities by the water companies is strongly supported by the NRA. It is encouraging that the sum total of the preliminary demand forecasts made by the water companies to the year 2014/15, as part of their 20 year asset management plans, is close to the NRA's Low demand scenario.

● Some doubts have been expressed regarding the long term savings in consumption which selective domestic metering will achieve. Similar uncertainty has also been expressed about the long term economic levels of leakage. It is vital that effort continues to demonstrate what demand management can or cannot achieve. Regular monitoring and reporting of demand management achievement will be undertaken by the NRA.

● The NRA does not claim to predict future demand levels with confidence and recognises that, however unlikely, water requirements could rise towards (or even exceed) the High demand scenario. This uncertainty, combined with the time likely to be needed to implement a given scheme means that steps must be taken now to investigate specific schemes and undertake the background work to facilitate scheme promotion. Not least will be the need for scheme promoters to undertake full environmental impact assessment of their proposals.

● The NRA should take a positive role in encouraging wise use of water by industry and other users across the community.

● Where the environmental impact of a scheme is uncertain the NRA should adopt a precautionary approach.

REGIONAL CONCLUSIONS

● Large scale transfers via the existing canal networks are not favoured as front runners within the strategy. Although the costs of improving the carrying capacity of relevant canals are relatively low it is the cost of bringing large scale water resources to the canals which makes this option less attractive. Canal transfers would also present some environmental difficulties, but providing these could be overcome it is possible that in the first instance they could be used for smaller scale transfers of perhaps of the order of 50 Ml/d.

● One of the primary issues resulting is the choice between the high cost but relatively low environmental impact, South West Oxfordshire reservoir scheme as against the cheaper but potentially high environmental impact River Severn to River Thames transfer scheme. Without such a transfer, future development for the Thames region would centre upon the South West Oxfordshire reservoir proposals and options for backup sources such as Vyrnwy redeployment or Craig Goch reservoir development would cease to be a serious consideration.

• The NRA believes that the possibility of a transfer of River Severn water into the River Thames is of such environmental and economic significance that a firm NRA position must be established in the near future.

• In the unlikely event that demands should rise towards the High scenario and if a River Severn to River Thames transfer is acceptable, the least cost sequence of resource development for meeting demands in the Thames (and Wessex) regions would be:

  a) construction of the River Severn to River Thames transfer taking unsupported flows from the River Severn (chosen on cost grounds);

  b) partial redeployment of Vyrnwy reservoir to support additional abstractions to the Thames, the Severn Trent and the Wessex regions as necessary (chosen on flexibility grounds);

  c) enlargement of Craig Goch reservoir for regulating the River Severn;

  d) construction of South West Oxfordshire reservoir.

• One major advantage associated with the above occurs in the longer term. The continued development of Shropshire groundwater to meet demands in the West Midlands and Wessex, together with the fact that the River Severn to River Thames transfer and Vyrnwy redeployment can be established relatively quickly, could postpone the need for the construction of large scale sources which may be under-utilised for decades due to lack of demand growth.

• Moreover, when a new resource is developed to further regulate the River Severn after the Shropshire scheme is fully committed, then it would be possible to rest this groundwater scheme in preference to any lower operating cost scheme which becomes available. Although the partial redeployment of Vyrnwy reservoir is selected in the above sequence of scheme development its use would depend upon the demand/resource balance in the North West region. The indication under the High demand scenario is that Vyrnwy would offer only a temporary resource for the River Severn, and if demands build up in the North West it would be preferable to reduce the regulation and increase the direct supply. In view of this it is likely that use of Vyrnwy for regulation should be viewed as a contingency resource to accommodate unexpected rates of demand growth upon the water resources of the River Severn.

• If a River Severn to River Thames transfer is not found to be acceptable then a piped transfer from the River Severn to London would warrant consideration before commitment is made to a South West Oxfordshire reservoir.

• To meet demands in East Anglia a reservoir or alternative development would be needed sometime between 2006 and 2011 according to the Medium scenario and between 1996 and 2006 for the High scenario. It is not possible at this stage to give a firm view on the most appropriate new water resources development to serve East Anglia. The full costs and environmental implications of the Fenland reservoir alternative to Great Bradley reservoir are not known but a preliminary view is that a reservoir option could be preferred to a transfer from the River Trent depending on the demand profile. This would be justified not only because of costs but also when operational risks and environmental issues are taken into account but there is a need for a closer examination of these issues.

● For the Severn Trent region the East Midlands is primarily supplied from the existing Carsington reservoir. In the High demand scenario Carsington reservoir is supported by abstractions from the River Trent and towards the end of the planning period the River Trent itself is supported by abstraction from the potential Birmingham rising groundwater source and also a new River Severn to River Trent transfer.

● Marginal demands in the West Midlands and Wessex region are expected to be met by increased regulation of the River Severn, primarily from continued development of the existing Shropshire groundwater scheme and if the High demand scenario arises an additional source will be needed in about 20 years time.

● If demands should unexpectedly rise towards the High demand scenario, it would not be possible to develop the Severn-Thames transfer or the South West Oxfordshire reservoir or the East Anglian reservoir in time, and therefore demand management would be the only realistic option available.

● The greatest need for additional agricultural water is likely to be in the Anglian region, largely for spray irrigation. Generally the NRA does not anticipate developing or financing schemes for particular classes of abstractor and the agricultural industry is no different in this respect. Opportunity exists for co-operation between agricultural abstractors to improve the management and allocation of existing abstraction rights together with joint ventures to develop new resources to meet specific agricultural needs. However water resource development is relatively expensive and may not be justified in many instances. Consideration could be given to buying into a scheme developed by a third party, either directly or through the NRA, but again the relative cost of such an alternative is unlikely to be justifiable in many cases. Clearly, if some agricultural demands were to be supplied from developments owned by the water companies then not only would the beneficiaries be expected to pay their proportion of costs but also the extra demand would bring forward the need for new developments.

● Regardless of the limited need for strategic development, local developments will be required to meet demonstrated need. Although the choice between local and strategic options is not part of this study, the large scale nature of strategic developments may in some instances be preferable to a number of smaller local developments. There appears to be much scope for these local developments. They include small inter regional transfers, local groundwater schemes, small abstractions and small reservoirs. Such opportunities clearly require further investigation.

8. FINANCE, PROMOTION AND DEVELOPMENT ROLES

Under Section 19 of the Water Resources Act 1991 the NRA has a duty to take action as and when it may consider necessary in order to conserve, redistribute or augment water resources and to ensure the proper use of such resources throughout England and Wales. The same legislation also states that the duties upon the NRA do not relieve the statutory water undertakers of the requirement to develop water resources to meet their obligations. The NRA's duty is therefore to ensure that the necessary conservation, redistribution and augmentation occurs - normally through developments undertaken by others - rather than to take action itself.

The NRA did however take responsibility for the ownership or operation of certain schemes when it was formed in 1989. These schemes were generally strategic regional developments which were used to meet the needs of a number of abstractors such as the Ely Ouse-Essex interbasin transfer scheme in East Anglia; the regulation of the River Severn using the Shropshire groundwater scheme; and the regulation of the River Itchen using the Candover groundwater scheme. These schemes are actually owned by the NRA, whereas other schemes are operated through agreements with water undertakers who manage river regulation systems such as the Kielder scheme in North East England and the Dee scheme in North Wales. Such schemes benefit abstractors, recreation, fisheries and the environment in general. Elsewhere, the NRA has negotiated agreements with water undertakers over storage to meet increased river regulation in the future.

The Government has indicated that it does not consider that the NRA should normally play a significant role in financing, developing or operating future new resources. Its role as "Guardian of the Water Environment" implies that it needs to act independently in assessing proposals and monitoring developments, as opposed to becoming an agent or operator arguing for a particular water resource option. The NRA's role can therefore be seen as one of ensuring that there is a balance between specific and possibly conflicting interests.

Current Government planning policy indicates that water resources considerations should not be used to directly limit or inhibit development. Providing that the environmental and other impacts on land-use are acceptable, water supply and sewerage developments will need to be undertaken. Nevertheless, developers will have to take account of the costs of ensuring environmentally acceptable water supplies and should also assess the on-costs to those who use their developments.

Significant investment in water resources schemes for water undertakers will almost certainly involve the participation of four parties. These are the water industry (since they will have to make the decision to invest), OFWAT (regarding the relationship between investment and the control of the industry's prices), the NRA (responsible for catchment management) and Government (for the necessary formal approvals).

Under the present water industry structure in England and Wales, the finance for water resources investment is expected to come from the private sector. The NRA has powers to install and operate water resources but it does not have powers to raise the finance for such activities except by means of abstraction charges. Therefore, capital finance could only come from direct payments from beneficiaries or from Government grants. However, Government have indicated that public financing is an ultimate fall-back option which could only be invoked if all other had been shown to be unworkable.

Major investments of this kind will clearly have implications for land-use planning. Planning authorities will therefore have a role to play in considering the implications of any water resources development proposals vis a vis land-use. This role is addressed in the Planning Policy Guidelines note on development plans. This document advises close consultation between planning authorities, water and sewerage undertakers and the NRA regarding the water-supply and sewerage infrastructure needed to support proposed development as well as the land required for that infrastructure.

In these circumstances, the final decisions on which water resources development schemes are preferred, (subject to the statutory controls), have to be made by the water undertakers who will be letting and financing the construction contracts. Within the general framework which will result from the NRA's resource planning work the initiative may lie with:

● An individual water company, either for its own needs or the requirements of others, or for both.

● A consortium of water companies, be they companies needing the water resources, or companies able to supply water resources, or a combination of both.

● Other private-sector investors who sees the bulk supply of water to a particular sector as a worthwhile area of business.

For the water undertakers, such decisions will have to be taken within the economic framework established by the Water Industry Act 1991 and the decisions of OFWAT.

The resulting arrangements will need to bear in mind the needs of water users outside the public supply system. This relates particularly to small users who will not be in a position to provide the substantial investments required for significant water resources schemes. The powers of the NRA to enter into water resource management schemes under Section 20 of the Water Resources Act 1991 are particularly significant for this purpose, but the NRA would expect the beneficiaries to meet the full cost of their share of the development.

It follows that the initiatives for proposing major water resources development schemes will normally lie with the water companies, be it individually or collectively in consortia. They will need to consult with the NRA and OFWAT in good time so as to demonstrate that their estimates of demand and timing are robust. They will also need to demonstrate that their longer-term plans for water-charging give appropriate weight to the volume of consumption and that day-to-day management measures to maximise existing resources have been exploited to an economically viable extent.

Therefore, the NRA's power to promote water resource schemes seems likely to be in the nature of a reserve power to be used when the initiative of water companies seems unlikely to ensure that major schemes are completed when and where required. Since the initiative will lie with the private sector, it must be for them to decide at what point they will promote a particular set of proposals. However, since such proposals may overlap or be inconsistent with each other, it is regarded as reasonable to expect those concerned to publicly indicate their intentions, in order that a systematic approach can be developed when considering the decisions needed on licences and orders. Regional discussions with the NRA would seem to be an effective means of enabling those concerned to reach conclusions on their intentions.

The opportunity to develop new water resources for the private abstractor requiring a relatively small abstraction is a potential difficulty. This is especially so in areas where local resources are already committed and would mostly apply to agricultural abstractions such as for spray irrigation. Issues relating to this have already been discussed in detail in section 3.5.4.

9. WAY FORWARD

The successful implementation of demand management strategies and the promotion of water efficiency are essential elements of the NRA strategy for the sustainable management of water resources. The NRA will therefore:

● reinforce its view to government that water companies and OFWAT should be given a statutory duty to promote the efficient use of water;

● require water companies to achieve economic levels of leakage and metering before new abstraction licences are granted for strategic developments;

● promote water efficiency in use in industry, commerce, agriculture and the home through the use of water audits, demonstration projects and advice;

● advise the government on the use of economic instruments including incentive charges and tradeable permits and promote changes in legislation to allow trials in selected catchments.

The NRA recognises the importance given to demand management by water companies and is encouraged that many water companies have identified targets for leakage control and selective domestic metering within their Asset Management Plan reviews which are consistent with the NRA's Low demand scenario. These targets will need to be backed up by investment agreed by OFWAT and monitored to ensure that real savings are achieved. There are however uncertainties that these levels of demand management are possible or cost effective and it will be important to identify preferred development options so that the strategy can be adjusted to meet increased demand should this be necessary.

In view of the uncertainties over the deficit forecasts and the time needed to promote a new resource, it is essential that the strategy for water resource development should be flexible. The aim should be to put forward a flexible programme of activities which will enable the water companies to meet their obligations to provide secure water supplies, whilst avoiding planning blight and abortive work on schemes which may never be required. Due to the probable long timescale for scheme completion, some activities should be put in hand as soon as possible as indicated below:

● baseline studies of the river corridors of the Severn and Thames as a forerunner to major environmental impact assessments of the river regulation and transfer schemes;

● review of the costs, benefits and environmental impact of key local development options together with a comparison to see whether any strategic developments would be preferred which could be developed in time;

● an investigation of the potential direct and indirect environmental impacts of redeploying Vyrnwy reservoir and of transferring water from the River Severn to the River Thames. Mitigation measures should be identified where possible;

● development of an inter-regional hydrological model which can simulate the operation of schemes transferring water between the Thames, Severn-Trent, Anglian and North West regions;

● research into the needs for minimum flows in rivers and to estuaries and development of an NRA policy for setting licence conditions for tidal limit abstractions. This would then be followed by the determination of prescribed flows for the strategic rivers - Thames, Severn, Trent and Ely Ouse.

The aim should be to complete these investigations within the next 5 years. By this time, there will be a clearer picture of the effectiveness of leakage control and water metering in the management of demand together with indication of the impact of the economy upon water demand.

During this 5 year period water companies will be encouraged to undertake pre-feasibility studies into their main options including environmental assessments. The NRA will also consult with companies over their plans for future development and liaise with companies, OFWAT and the DoE on issues related to the co-ordination, funding and promotion of large strategic schemes. At the same time others in the private sector may come forward with their own proposals for consideration by water companies and the NRA.

The agricultural demand for water, especially for spray irrigation, present particular problems for the provision of future supplies. The widespread demand in eastern England and the lack of a suitable infrastructure for distribution means it is difficult to make a strategic resource available to a large number of users over a wide area. The NRA has therefore promoted the need for the NRA, MAFF and other interested organisations to establish the institutional framework to promote the economic development and improved management of resources for the agricultural sector. MAFF has agreed to make the necessary arrangements which are to commence in 1994. A forum of the key parties will be established and will consider relevant issues including:

● the scope for including an allowance for agricultural (spray irrigation) demand in strategic developments;

● the financing of economic developments by the agricultural sector;

● opportunities for improved water conservation and use at a local level;

● the need to develop and explain policy.

More generally, the NRA will need to develop a better understanding of the environmental value of habitats and species so that more informed decisions can be taken on which parts of the environment are 'tradeable' and which must be protected 'at all costs'.

REFERENCES:

1. Binnie, C.J.A, Herrington, P.J (1992) *Effects of Climate Change on Water Resources and Demands* (Unpublished paper, June 1992)

2. Department of the Environment (1992a) *Using Water Wisely - A Consultation Paper* (DoE, London)

3. Department of the Environment (1992b) *Digest of Environmental Protection and Water Statistics* No. 15 (HMSO, London)

4. NRA (1992a) *NRA Water Resources Development Strategy - A Discussion Document* (National Rivers Authority, Bristol)

5. NRA (1992b) *NRA Groundwater Protection Policy* (National Rivers Authority, Bristol)

6. NRA (1993) *NRA Water Resources Strategy* (National Rivers Authority, Bristol)

7. Parliamentary Office of Science & Technology (1993) *Dealing with Drought - Environmental & Technical Aspects of Water Shortages* (POST, London)

8. Rees, J & Williams, S (1993) *Water for Life - Strategies for Sustainable Water Resource Management* (C.P.R.E., London)

9. Weatherhead, E.K, Place, A.J, Morris, J, Burton, M, (1993) *Demand for Irrigation Water* (R&D Report 14, National Rivers Authority, Bristol)

ADDITIONAL KEY RELATED PUBLICATIONS

1) Department of the Environment (1993) *UK Strategy for Sustainable Development Consultation Paper* (DoE, London)

2) Department of the Environment (1994) *Sustainable Development The UK Strategy* (HMSO, London)

3) Office of Water Services (1992) *The Cost of Water Delivered to Customers 1991 - 1992 - A comparison of unit costs and of losses from companies distribution systems* (OFWAT, Birmingham)

4) Water Resources Board (1973) *Water Resources in England and Wales* Volumes 1 & 2 (HMSO, London)

APPENDIX 1: LOCAL RESOURCE DEVELOPMENT OPTIONS INCLUDED IN THE MARGINAL DEMAND ANALYSIS

(Note: Inclusion of schemes does not necessarily mean that they would be supported by the NRA or that the yields are definitive).

Location	Development		Assumed Yield (Ml/d)
Anglian	Chalk Groundwater		40
	Increased abstraction from the Trent		36
	Chelmsford effluent re-use		50
		TOTAL	126
Northumbria	Magnesian Limestone SE Durham		8
	Unallocated Kielder		13
		TOTAL	21
North West	Ribble Pumped Storage (Rivington)		40
	Huntington Treatment Works Expansion		74
	Windermere Group Increase to Licence Quantity		10
	Lancashire Conjunctive Use Scheme Developments		80
	Improvements to existing Groundwater schemes		17
		TOTAL	221
Severn-Trent	West Shropshire Area Developments		34
	East Shropshire Area Developments		12
	Wolverhampton Area Developments		14
	Worcester Area Developments		2
	Gloucester Area Developments		6
	South Warks/Coventry Area Developments		21
	Stoke Area Developments		15
	South Staffs Area Developments		37
	Trent/Carsington Conjunctive Use		60
	Shropshire groundwater (including re-use element)		150
		TOTAL	351
Southern	Havant Thicket Reservoir		30
	Yalding Minor Works		29
	Local Groundwater (net increase)		6
	Darwell Reservoir		42
	Rother - Medway Link		2
	Crowhurst Bridge		4
	Chillerton Reservoir		9
	Rother - Medway Link		2
	Test Groundwater Scheme		25
	River Itchen development		48
	Testwood lakes		5
	Local reallocations using Itchen yield		22
	Broad Oak Reservoir development		40
		TOTAL	264

Location	Development	Assumed Yield (Ml/d)
South West	Wimbleball pumped storage	30
	Roadford pumped storage	50
	Colliford pumped storage	50
	TOTAL	130
Thames	Increase in existing supply from Grafham	45
	Thames side Groundwater - Harpsden	10
	Thames side Groundwater - Reading	20
	Thames side Groundwater - Remenham	10
	Thames side Groundwater - West Marlow	10
	Rising Groundwater - London	30
	Artificial Recharge North London	90
	Artificial Recharge South London	90
	TOTAL	305
Welsh	Local supplies in Hereford & Radnor	20
	Local Supplies in North Dyfed area	10
	Local supplies in Merionnydd	20
	Llyn Celyn Developments	20
	Dee Developments	21
	Brianne Phase II	127
	TOTAL	218
Wessex	River Avon at Bath	55
	Wimbleball Pumped Storage	10
	Shropshire Groundwater (Bristol)	55
	TOTAL	120
Yorkshire	Local Groundwater Developments	20
	Groundwater Developments - York	35
	River Ouse Licence Changes	30
	River Aire Developments	50
	Washburn Valley Developments	50
	Operational Changes	50
	Tees transfer from Kielder	60
	TOTAL	295
	GRAND TOTAL	2051

APPENDIX 2: KEY STRATEGIC RESOURCE OPTIONS AND TRANSFER LINKS

A2.1
RIVER SEVERN TO RIVER THAMES TRANSFER

A2.1.1
Option Description

The Severn to Thames transfer scheme (see Figures A2.1 and A2.2) involves abstracting water from the River Severn in the vicinity of Deerhurst in the lower reaches of the river, and discharging it in the vicinity of Buscot in the upper Thames. The Thames would then be used as a natural conduit to convey these additional resources towards London where the water would be transferred into existing reservoirs.

The following subsections relate to the river-to-river transfer, but in addition outline consideration has been given to an option in which water from the River Severn in the vicinity of Deerhurst is piped directly to the supply areas in the Thames region rather than into the River Thames itself. This would involve a pipeline some 90 Km in length terminating in the London area. Preliminary capital costs of a 200 Ml/d transfer have been estimated at £117M. This option would have the advantage that it would avoid potential environmental problems associated with the mixing of 'foreign' water with water in the River Thames but has the disadvantages of being more expensive than the river-to-river alternative and potential difficulties which could be associated with different source water qualities being fed into distribution systems.

Returning to the river-to-river transfer option bankside storage would be provided at Deerhurst to allow some settlement of suspended solids, and to act as a buffer against pollution incidents in the River Severn. Storage would also be provided near the Thames end of the transfer, for blending and operational control purposes. Such storage could be provided by developing and using gravel pits, already identified in the Gloucestershire Minerals Plan, close to Down Ampney. The transfer itself would be effected primarily by pipeline although there are advantages in incorporating a part of the Thames and Severn Canal into the route between Eysey Lock (near Down Ampney) and Inglesham Lock at the River Thames.

Water could only be made available in the River Severn subject to a prescribed flow below which no abstraction would be allowed in order to protect the downstream environment. Water above the prescribed flow could be made available in the following ways:

i)
Without Additional Regulation of River Severn

Abstractions could be made at times of higher flows in the River Severn, and water pumped to the River Thames and subsequently stored in the London reservoirs. This option provides only limited additional resources, but could be a relatively low-cost solution to slowly increasing demand and could form the first stage of a subsequent enhanced transfer. The reliable yield could be up to 146 Ml/d and the capital cost would be £57M or £92M for a 200 Ml/d or 400 Ml/d transfer capacity respectively.

ii)

With Additional Regulation based upon an Enlarged Craig Goch Reservoir

There is considerable scope to enlarge the existing Craig Goch Reservoir in the Elan Valley (a tributary of the River Wye in mid-Wales). This scheme was extensively investigated in the 1970s, when a number of sub-options of varying complexity were identified. An enlarged reservoir, with a top water level 49 m higher than the present level and storage of 190,000 Ml, could be used to regulate the River Severn at times of low flow via a tunnel discharging at Llanidloes (see Figure A2.1). The reliable yield could be up to 775 Ml/d and the capital cost would be £105M assuming the water was used for regulation of the Severn.

As an alternative, the enlarged reservoir could be used to regulate low flows in the River Wye; in this case regulation releases would be made via a tunnel to the Wye above Rhayader and abstraction for transfer to the River Thames would be at an intake in the vicinity of Ross-on-Wye. The pipeline from the River Wye would cross the River Severn in the vicinity of Deerhurst and then follow the route which the Severn to Thames transfer described above would take (see Figure A2.1). These options could support flows in the River Severn to meet demands in the Wessex area. The capital cost of an enlarged Craig Goch used to regulate the Wye would be £72M.

iii)

With Additional Regulation based upon a Partially Redeployed Vyrnwy Reservoir

The existing Vyrnwy reservoir in mid-Wales lies on a tributary to the River Severn but is currently used as a direct supply source for Liverpool, with water being transferred northwards by gravity along the Vyrnwy aqueduct (see Figure A2.1). The reservoir could be partially redeployed to regulate the Severn in the same way as the existing Clywedog reservoir. For operational reasons the existing direct supply cannot be reduced below 60 Ml/d. The Vyrnwy option would require capital expenditure both to uprate some existing sources and possibly for the development of replacement sources in the North West. Outlet arrangements at Vyrnwy would also need to be modified. In addition, operating costs would increase for North West Water Ltd resulting from the loss of the cheaper gravity supply from Vyrnwy reservoir and the extra costs of treating additional lowland river water from the River Dee. The additional yield which would be released for regulation of the Severn by partial redeployment could be up to 147 Ml/d and could have a capital cost of £42M, depending upon timing and demands. When used to regulate the River Severn and/or River Thames this yield can be increased.

The effects of increased regulation of the River Severn or River Wye (these rivers are already regulated), would need to be closely examined and reviewed in the light of similar operational experiences elsewhere. Environmental mitigation measures would need to be considered where these are viable and the possibility of a pipeline to London, instead of the use of the River Thames, could not be ruled out should mixing different river waters present an unacceptable environmental risk.

Figure A2.1

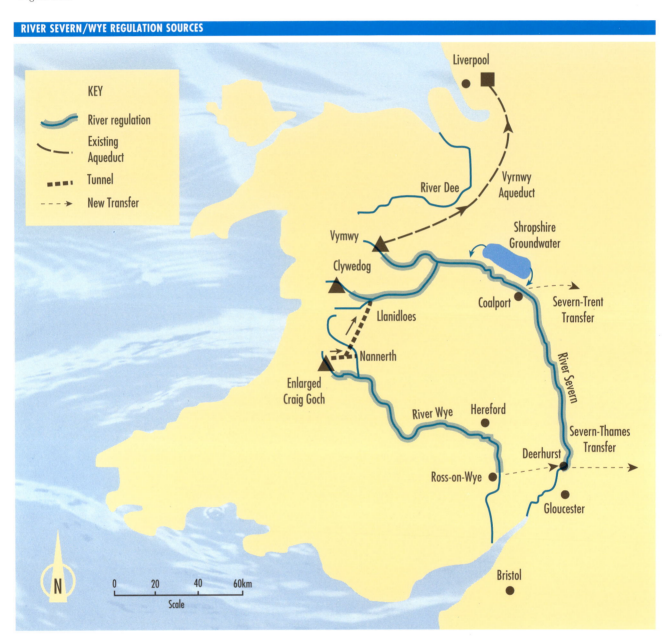

RIVER SEVERN/WYE REGULATION SOURCES

KEY
- River regulation
- Existing Aqueduct
- Tunnel
- New Transfer

Liverpool

River Dee

Vyrnwy Aqueduct

Vymwy

Clywedog

Shropshire Groundwater

Llanidloes

Coalport

Severn-Trent Transfer

Nannerth

Enlarged Craig Goch

River Wye

Hereford

River Severn

Ross-on-Wye

Deerhurst

Severn-Thames Transfer

Gloucester

Bristol

N

0   20   40   60km
Scale

A2.1.2

Environmental Issues

The environmental issues associated with this option relate both to the actual transfer and, when needed, the sources of water for additional regulation of the Severn.

i)

Transfer

The key issues associated with the environmental impacts of a River Severn to River Thames transfer relate to the water quality and biological impacts of transferring water from the downstream end of a large lowland river into the upstream end of the River Thames - particularly during low flow periods in the Thames. Further investigation of this issue is required before this scheme can be considered for promotion.

There is also concern over potential disruption to upstream salmon migration in the River Severn. However, the abstraction at Deerhurst would be subject to a prescribed flow (PF) below which no abstraction would be allowed, and other flow regime restrictions as shown to be necessary to protect the downstream environment and ensure that there is no adverse impact on salmon migration. A PF of 2,500 Ml/d has been proposed which, from the investigations to date, would appear to be sufficient to prevent any significant environmental risks although there is still some concern over the flow required to protect salmonid migration.

The final route of the transfer pipeline may need to be adjusted to take account of a number of nature conservation or archaeological constraints along the route, but any impacts would be largely temporary and confined to the construction phase. Use of the currently derelict Thames & Severn Canal for the last section of the transfer route would however, provide considerable potential for environmental and recreational benefit.

ii)
Enlarged Craig Goch Reservoir

Enlargement of Craig Goch reservoir can be achieved by construction of a comparatively small new dam at the downstream narrow neck of a wide, long valley. The development would not have any significant community or archaeological impacts due to the remoteness of the area, but it would result in inundation of part of the Elenydd SSSI and other sites of nature conservation value. Any proposals affecting Elenydd and associated habitats would be of particular concern to the NRA and are likely to receive strong objections from the Countryside Council for Wales due to their national and possibly international importance.

Regulation of the River Severn with water from the enlarged reservoir would be in addition to that currently made from Clywedog and to a lesser extent Vyrnwy reservoir. The effects of additional regulation would need to be evaluated and the loss of water from the Wye catchment would also need careful consideration.

Further regulation of the River Wye on the other hand raises a number of concerns since the whole river, including the riparian habitats, has been classified as a SSSI and as such is of national value.

The Wye is also a very important salmon river. Although river flows are already affected by impoundments in the headwaters and periodic regulation releases, there is concern that the salmonid spawning reaches of the upper Wye may be affected by an altered flow regime. At the same time, however, moderation of extreme low flows may provide benefits in terms of reduced environmental risk and improved habitat stability.

iii)
Redeployed Vyrnwy Reservoir

The key issues of concern associated with the partial redeployment of Vyrnwy Reservoir from direct supply for Liverpool to regulation of the River Severn relate to the potential impacts on the flora and fauna of the River Vyrnwy, particularly the salmonid nursery areas.

The redeployment proposals would serve to exacerbate low flows, although the upper flow regime would remain essentially unaltered. Concern is centred, therefore, on the maintenance of stable nursery areas without excessive washout.

There is also concern over possible water quality and/or temperature problems arising from the release of water from the lower levels of the reservoir. However, any impacts could be mitigated through construction of new, multiple-level drawoff facilities, although this may take the reservoir out of operation for a period of time.

In addition, the implications of developing alternative water sources within the North West to replace the direct supply from Vyrnwy will need to be examined if this option is to be promoted.

A2.2.
SOUTH WEST OXFORDSHIRE RESERVOIR

A2.2.1
Option Description

Proposals to construct a major new pumped storage reservoir in South West Oxfordshire have been under active investigation by Thames Water Utilities and the NRA. The scheme, as originally proposed, would be one of the largest reservoir developments in England providing operational capacity up to 150,000Ml. Abstraction from the River Thames to fill the reservoir would be restricted to periods of high river flows, largely during the winter months. Stored water would be used in two ways: to provide a continuous treated supply to the Upper Thames area; and to support abstractions for the London supply reservoirs by augmentation of the River Thames during drier periods. For a reliable yield of up to 350 Ml/d the capital cost would be in the region of £400M.

The scheme could also be operated in conjunction with a River Severn to River Thames transfer (see Figure A2.2) to meet potentially high demands at some stage beyond the current planning horizon.

A2.2.2
Environmental Issues

Construction of this scheme would require extensive landtake, approximately 14sq. Km. However, the agricultural land classification is largely grade 3 and the impacts are considered to be low to moderate. Because the scheme would need to be an embanked construction with bunds up to 25m above ground level, the visual impacts will be significant.

The area is currently overlooked by the higher ground of the Berkshire Downs and there are three small villages in very close proximity to the proposed site. A number of small water courses which currently cross the site would need to be redirected.

There would be considerable local disturbance during construction through traffic, noise and dust during earthworking. Additional risks to the water environment may also arise through sediment disturbance, runoff from the construction area and possible pollution by fuel oils stored on site. Many of these effects could be mitigated through advanced planting (tree lines) and

Figure A2.2

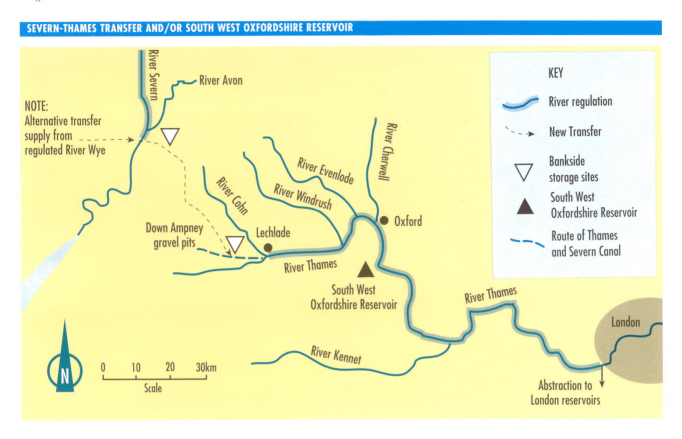

SEVERN-THAMES TRANSFER AND/OR SOUTH WEST OXFORDSHIRE RESERVOIR

consideration given to the final design at an early stage; for example, developing settlement lagoons which could be later redesigned as wetland conservation areas.

Due to the current intensive agricultural use of the proposed site, the impact on nature conservation is considered to be limited. The operation of the scheme, however, may have potential implications for downstream water meadows alongside the River Thames which rely on seasonal inundation.

Additional effects of operation on the aquatic ecology of the River Thames are currently being investigated. Key issues include the potential effects on fisheries and riverine habitats and the inter-relationship between reservoir and river algal assemblages. These issues are the subject of further investigation aimed at identifying constraints on operation which would need to be included within Licence and Operating Agreements.

If designed appropriately, a number of environmental enhancements could be created in and around the proposed scheme. The reservoir itself could provide considerable recreational and conservation potential and significant peripheral environmental enhancements could be developed. In addition, the scheme could be operated in conjunction with some existing sources to alleviate impacts of abstraction at times of low flows. The development of this scheme in advance of a Severn to Thames transfer would provide an opportunity, should the need ever arise, to transfer water directly into storage, allowing mixing with River Thames derived water and alleviating the potential environmental effects of releasing River Severn water directly into the River Thames.

A2.3
RIVER SEVERN TO RIVER TRENT TRANSFER

A2.3.1
Option Description

The River Severn to River Trent transfer scheme involves abstracting water from the River Severn in the vicinity of Coalport in the middle reaches of the river, and discharging it around the confluence of the River Sow and the River Trent, east of Stafford. Various routes and pipeline capacities have been investigated; a 300Ml/d capacity transfer with a capital cost of £70M would probably be piped all the way to the River Trent whereas a 100 Ml/d transfer with a capital cost of £26M could be piped to lower Drayton on the River Penk which would then serve as a natural pipeline to convey the transfer water to the River Sow and then to the Trent (see FigureA2.3). Balancing storage would be provided near the Trent end of the transfer for operation control purposes.

This transfer could be used to regulate the Trent to help supply the East Midlands demand centres and/or to support further transfer of water from the lower reaches of the Trent to the Anglian region. It could also be used to supply water to the canal system for onward transfer to the Thames or Anglian regions. Modelling studies have shown that increased regulation of the River Severn would be needed to support this transfer - this could be provided from the Craig Goch or Vyrnwy options discussed earlier.

A2.3.2
Environmental Issues

This option could lead to high local impacts on the flow regime in the Rivers Penk and Sow. This could have a detrimental impact on the aquatic ecology of these rivers although the existing biological quality is only moderate to low. Water quality on the other hand may benefit from the transfer of National Water Council (NWC) Class 1B river Severn water into the lower quality, Class 2 river Penk, Sow and Trent. There is, however, some concern over the possible transfer of the fish disease Pomphorhynchus to the River Trent which is known to affect chub, barbel and other species. The potential impacts associated with construction of the pipeline are predominantly temporary and relate to construction activity. Therefore, provided the final pipeline route is planned to avoid any site specific planning constraints and appropriate post-construction habitat restoration is undertaken, this option seems to have low environmental risks. With regard to the abstraction from the River Severn the main concern relates to ensuring that upstream salmonid migration is not disrupted, although with the flows under consideration this is not considered likely to be a major problem.

Figure A2.3

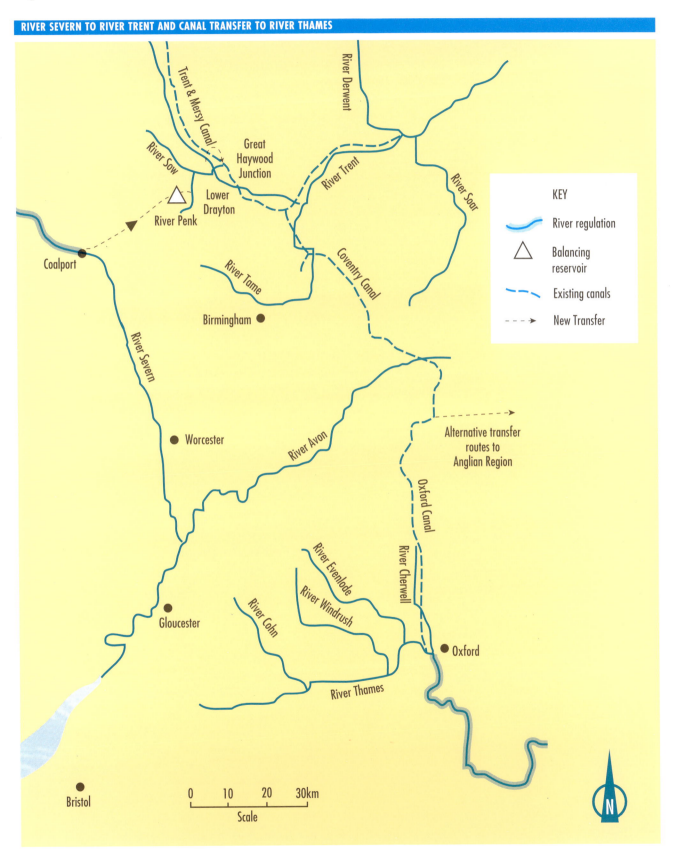

A2.4
CANAL TRANSFER TO THE THAMES AND ANGLIAN REGIONS

A2.4.1
Option Description

Water would be abstracted from the River Severn in the vicinity of Coalport and taken along the route of the Severn to Trent transfer described above to the Trent and Mersey Canal at Great Hayward Junction. From there water can be transferred to the River Thames at Oxford via the Trent and Mersey, Coventry and Oxford Canals (see Figure A2.3). Ascending lock flights would need to be bypassed via pumping mains, and some additional capital works such as dredging and bank raising would be needed in places to improve conveyance whilst safeguarding the interests of other canal users. A transfer capacity of 100 Ml/d would have a capital cost of approximately £49.1M.

Further options to deliver water by canal to East Anglian rivers also exist. A further possibility is to use part of the existing Vyrnwy aqueduct or rising groundwater around Birmingham as a means of supplying the canal system with additional water for transfer.

A2.4.2
Environmental Issues

The key issue of concern related to the transfer of water by canals is the potential for water quality problems arising from the discharge of poor quality (often eutrophic) canal water into the recipient rivers such as the Thames. In some cases, however, the quality of the canal water itself may actually be improved due to the addition of higher quality transfer water. However infrequent use may mean poor quality water impacting on rivers at critical times.

In order to facilitate the transfer of the additional flows, the canals may need to be dredged which could have adverse impacts on the instream ecology and fisheries of the canals, some reaches of which are designated SSSIs. There will also be a need for some construction work which will create short-term disruption. In the long-term there may be amenity and recreational benefits.

A2.5
EAST ANGLIAN RESERVOIR

A2.5.1
Option Description

This option relates to one of two possible new reservoir sites in East Anglia to operate in conjunction with the existing Ely Ouse-Essex transfer system. This would augment water supplies to much of Essex and elsewhere and add security to water resources in the south of the region (see Figure A2.4). Either reservoir could be filled just by surplus winter flows in the River Ouse at Denver or, additionally, by water transferred from the River Trent.

A potential site for a new reservoir has been identified at Great Bradley just south of Newmarket, and detailed feasibility studies have been carried out. The alternative is located on the Fens close to the existing pumping station transferring water from the Ely Ouse to Essex. The Fenland site has been identified by Essex Water Company but investigations are currently only at an early stage. The reliable yield for Great Bradley is up to 268 Ml/d, but is dependent on reservoir capacity and input pump size. However, for a yield of 174 Ml/d the reservoir capacity would be 46 million cubic metres and the existing Ely Ouse-Essex pumps at Kennet would need a capacity of 681 Ml/d. For this combination the capital cost would be in the order of £69.4M. The yield of the Fenland reservoir is under investigation.

A2.5.2

Environmental Issues

The environmental implications of Great Bradley have been examined in some detail whereas investigations into the alternative Fenland site are at a very early stage and the environmental impacts still need to be examined. The Fenland site near Feltwell would require the construction of a bunded reservoir; a preliminary view is that it would be relatively expensive to construct and may have fewer environmental issues than the Great Bradley site.

At Great Bradley the likely impacts are dependent on the size of reservoir developed. The largest potential reservoir, with a top water level of 105.5 mAOD would result in the partial loss of four ancient woodland SSSIs and a further five ancient woodlands of nature conservation value. In addition, 53 residential properties would be inundated including 5 listed buildings, and 17 sites of archaeological interest would be affected. It is therefore, considered that this size of reservoir would be difficult to promote. A smaller reservoir, with a top water level of say 99.1 mAOD, would have a lesser impact, inundating 21 properties although some of the woodland sites would still be affected.

Other potentially adverse effects could arise on the siltation pattern, water quality, fisheries and ecology of the tidal Ely Ouse and the Wash Estuary SSSI/RAMSAR site due to a reduction in winter flows. Regulation releases from the reservoir to the rivers Stour and Pant would result in a much steadier rate of transfer down those rivers which may improve the current flow regime, water quality and in-stream ecology.

There would obviously be temporary impacts during the construction stages, but once completed the reservoir would provide significant long term recreation opportunities and would also provide a considerable conservation resource in its own right.

Figure A2.4

TRENT-ANGLIAN TRANSFER AND/OR EAST ANGLIAN RESERVOIR OPTIONS

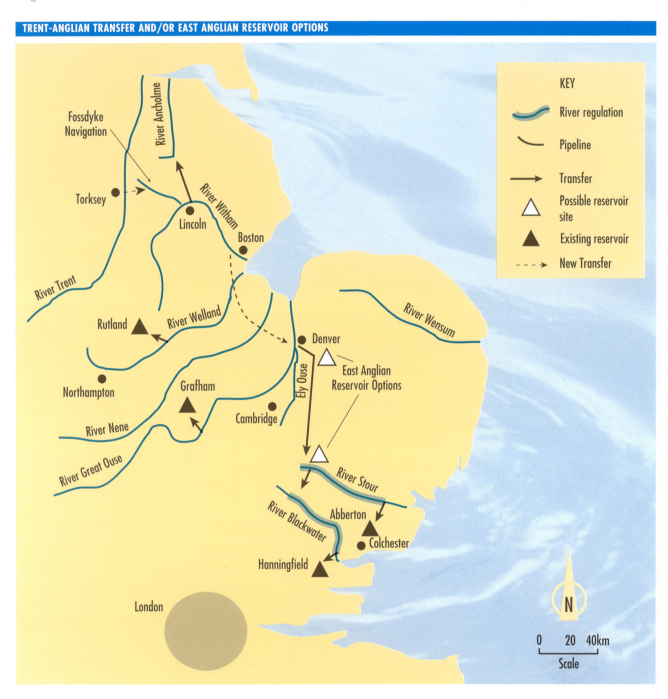

A2.6
UNSUPPORTED RIVER TRENT TO ANGLIAN TRANSFER

A2.6.1
Option Description

This option involves the abstraction of surplus water from the Lower Trent at Torksey subject to the protection of a prescribed flow below which no abstraction would be allowed in order to protect the downstream environment. This water could then be transferred through the Trent - Fossdyke pipeline (part of the existing Trent-Witham-Ancholme scheme which supplies water to the Grimsby and Scunthorpe areas) to the River Witham and then through a new pipeline to the existing Ely Ouse-Essex transfer system to meet demands in Essex (see Figure A2.4).

Such a transfer could either be operated alone or in conjunction with a new East Anglian Reservoir as described above. For a 200 Ml/d capacity transfer the indicative capital cost is £108M.

A2.6.2
Environmental Issues

The environmental implications of this option operating alone have been examined. Further studies would be required to examine any differences in the impacts that might arise if the scheme were operated in conjunction with a new reservoir.

The principal issue of concern in relation to this option relates to water quality. Although transfer of Trent water through the large fen drain sections of the Witham and Ancholme is a long established practice, its introduction into the more sensitive fluvial rivers Stour and Blackwater would require further investigation. There is concern that proposed flue gas desulphurisation at some Trent power stations could significantly increase sulphate and metal concentrations in the Trent, but this could be controlled by appropriate conditions on consents to discharge.

Apart from the concerns over water quality, it is not generally envisaged that there would be any significantly detrimental impacts arising from this scheme although consideration would need to be given to the level of prescribed flow which would be required at Torksey to protect the downstream environment of the Trent and Humber Estuary. There is also some concern over possible disruption to fisheries in the Fossdyke Navigation and River Witham, both during any construction required to accommodate the increased flow (minor bank protection, alternation to bridges and locks and dredging works, etc), and arising from the actual transfer of large, intermitted volumes. However, provided any construction work is carefully controlled, the general indication is that the environmental risks associated with these issues can be considered low.

A2.7
BIRMINGHAM
RISING GROUNDWATER

A2.7.1
Option Description

Due to declining industrial abstraction in the Birmingham area, groundwater levels have been rising. In the region of 50 Ml/d abstraction with a capital cost of £4.4M appears possible from the groundwaters below Birmingham although this is currently the subject of a feasibility study. The strategy has included this source as an option for augmentation of the River Trent or canal system.

A2.7.2
Environmental Issues

Addition of Birmingham groundwater to the rivers feeding the Trent - such as the River Rea and River Tame - is likely to provide an environmental benefit through improvement in the existing poor water quality of these rivers. Concerns over the continued rise of groundwater into localised contaminated land will be alleviated by an abstraction scheme and ensure that surface water quality will be unaffected from this additional source of pollution. Chlorinated solvent pollution of some groundwater may pose limitations in discharge to surface watercourses, but provided adequate operating and monitoring controls are put in place, should not be a significant problem.

APPENDIX 3: ENVIRONMENTAL IMPLICATIONS OF KEY STRATEGIC RESOURCE OPTIONS AND TRANSFER LINKS

A3.1

INTRODUCTION

In examining the environmental implications of the national water resource development strategy due account has been taken of the NRA's role as "Guardian of the Water Environment". Assessment of the potential environmental effects of strategic water resource development options has formed a key part of the strategy process, aimed at identifying those options which appear to have least potential for adverse impact, and provide most opportunities for the enhancement of the aquatic environment. *This work is just a starting point and the options will require a considerably greater level of detailed study and investigation in the future, before any firm decision can be made as to whether or not, and in what form, they can be approved for implementation.*

A3.2

ROLE OF ENVIRONMENTAL ASSESSMENT

Environmental Impact Assessment (EIA) is the process of identifying, predicting and evaluating the impact of particular activities on the environment, the conclusions of which are used as a tool in decision making. It has been applied at an individual strategic option level during studies carried out on a regional basis.

There has also been a need for a higher level comparative assessment in the planning and appraisal process. For the purposes of this strategy, an intermediate level of environmental assessment between Strategic Environmental Assessment and detailed project specific Environmental Assessment has been undertaken at a preliminary level, examining the strategic development options and their components on as comparable and objective basis as possible, based on presently available information.

Strategic Environmental Assessment (SEA) may be defined as the systematic and comprehensive process of evaluating the environmental impacts of a policy, plan or programme and its alternatives. It enables relevant environmental issues, objectives and constraints to be more fully involved at an early planning stage and assists in implementing the concept of sustainability.

Environmental sustainability has many definitions, but they all include the notion of the continuity of a resource base over time. For the present strategy it implies there should be no long-term systematic deterioration in the water environment due to resource development, and equates to the NRA's mission to protect and improve the environment. Since the Brundtland Commission's report in 1987, sustainability has become accepted as a goal of many environmental policies.

Strategic Environmental Assessment may be seen as an integral step in the attainment of sustainability, by broadening the remit of EIA upwards from projects to plans and policies, and defining the acceptable limits of change. Its application to the development of a water resources development strategy lies principally in its ability to identify the least environmentally sustainable schemes, and thus to enable attention to be concentrated on more acceptable plan formulations. The initial broad application of a strategic evaluation also serves to identify areas where further information is required for the environmental assessment.

The UK has no formal procedure for SEA. The Department of the Environment's guide *Policy Appraisal and the Environment* (1991) presents administrative guidance. The guide recognises that the environmental effects of policy must be taken into account in government policy making. *It stresses the need to adopt a precautionary approach due to the high level of uncertainty of impact prediction.* However, the methodologies proposed are more applicable to the assessment of policies than the plan framework of the present project. Planning Policy Guidance note 12 (DoE 1992a) also goes some way to giving guidance on strategic environmental planning. In 1991 the European Community has recently proposed a new Directive for the application of SEA to certain policies, plans and programmes.

There are a number of constraints to strategic EA at the planning level, including the nebulous nature of the proposals, lack of information regarding projected conditions, lack of precision of impact prediction, and the large number and variety of alternatives.

A3.3
METHOD OF ASSESSING ENVIRONMENTAL IMPLICATIONS

The basic unit of assessment has been taken to be the components which make up each strategic resource development option. The components have been defined as:

River reaches }
Canal reaches } in which aquatic issues dominate

Reservoirs }
Pipelines } in which general planning issues dominate

The assessment matrices for these two groups of components differ due to the nature of the impacts. A series of preliminary assessment framework tables has been produced for rivers and canals; and likewise a corresponding set of tables for reservoirs and pipelines (see tables A3.1 to A3.4).

The potential for environmental impacts depends upon:

● the sensitivity of the site/receptors;

● the risk of significant environmental change/damage;

● the expected magnitude and duration of change;

● the potential for mitigation.

A further important factor considered in the assessment has been the opportunity for improvement or benefits associated with the option.

The categorisation of impacts and criteria for assessing their severity follows directly from the key issues and criteria described in the next section. For rivers and canals, aquatic issues are most important, and the categories used have been the general character of the reach; existing water quality; fisheries status; aquatic ecology; terrestrial ecology; recreation/amenity/navigation; and general land-use/planning issues. For reservoirs and pipelines, planning issues are of primary importance. The categories used have been general character of the landscape; agricultural land; existing archaeology and cultural heritage; terrestrial ecology; recreation and amenity opportunities; and general land-use/planning issues.

For every component of each strategic resource development option the existing sensitivity of each of these categories has been designated as "high", "moderate" or "low", using the criteria shown in Table A3.1 for rivers and canals, and Table A3.2 for reservoirs and pipelines. In general, receptors of national importance or with statutory protection have been deemed to be of high sensitivity.

The assessment of risk has been made in a similar manner. Risk is the potential for adverse change or impact consequent upon the development, and may be short term (only experienced during construction) or long term (experienced when the scheme is operational). The "high" and "moderate" risks adopted for use in this assessment are given in Table A3.3 for rivers/canals and Table A3.4 for reservoirs/pipelines.

The complexity of aquatic and terrestrial ecological systems is such that the effects of particular impacts on the functioning of these systems are not yet fully understood. It is therefore difficult to define specific thresholds above which impacts can be defined as significant or unsustainable. The criteria shown in Tables A3.3 and A3.4 are a preliminary attempt to be as rigorous and consistent as possible when comparing the effects of quite different components and overall schemes studied to differing levels of detail.

In the assessment of risk, it has been assumed that the water transfers will occur as planned and modelled in the individual scheme-specific Environmental Assessments. Where specific hydrological data were lacking, a preliminary analysis has been performed using data extracted from the Institute of Hydrology (1993) summary of Hydrological Statistics 1986-1990.

A3.4
CRITERIA FOR ASSESSING
ENVIRONMENTAL IMPLICATIONS

For the high-level environmental assessment of the potential environmental consequences of strategic resource developments, key environmental issues have been identified together with criteria for assigning sensitivity and risk to components of water resource developments. The issues and criteria have been derived from literature reviews, information on the actual impacts of existing UK schemes and specific project and environmental studies undertaken for the strategy. Key issues and criteria are summarised below by category:

Landscape/General Character
Water Quality
Fisheries
Aquatic Ecology

Terrestrial Ecology
Agricultural Land
Archaeology and Cultural Heritage
Recreation, Amenity and Navigation

LANDSCAPE/
GENERAL CHARACTER

At this intermediate level of environmental assessment the evaluation of the impact of reservoirs, pipelines or changes arising from alterations to the flow regime of rivers or canals has been based on the landscape designation of the area. High adverse impacts are liable to arise in nationally designated sites, i.e. National Parks, National Heritage Areas, Heritage Coasts, Areas of Outstanding Natural Beauty, National Scenic Areas and National Trust sites. County or local classifications, such as Areas of Great Landscape Value, Special Areas of Great Landscape Value, Regional or Country Parks and Green Belt areas will be subject to moderate impacts.

Certain developments may have beneficial impacts, particularly valley-site reservoirs as opposed to bunded impoundments, and the landscape quality may be improved where river regulation maintains higher flows in rivers subject to low flow problems due to over-abstraction.

WATER QUALITY

The water quality of all rivers in the UK is defined by the National Water Council (NWC) classification, which provides a basis for defining both sensitivity and risk. Any development which is liable to result in a fall in quality from Class 1A or 1B, or which breaches the proposed Statutory Water Quality Objectives under Section 83 of the Water Resources Act 1991, when formally introduced, is considered to have a high risk. A development which creates or increases the frequency of algal blooms, or increases nutrient status, is considered to be of moderate risk.

FISHERIES

The principal impacts relating to fisheries arise from changes in flow, water chemistry and temperature, and the risk of transfer of alien species and diseases. The significance of the impact will depend on the sensitivity and value of the fisheries, and the magnitude of the potential change. High adverse impacts are considered to arise from:

● the loss of freshets or spate flows affecting migratory salmonids;

● the physical restriction to movement of migratory species;

● the reduction in flow velocity affecting species with specific flowing water requirements, especially salmonids, chubb, dace and barbel;

● a fall in NWC class or exceedence of the threshold level for any European Inland Fisheries Advisory Commission (EIFAC) parameter;

● the transfer of category A pathogens (notifiable diseases) or category B if their incidence in the recipient river is potentially damaging;

● the transfer of alien species;

The following impacts are considered to be moderate in terms of their risk:

● increased duration of velocities outside the species preference;

● fish impingement in intakes;

● temperature changes due to mixing or reservoir releases;

● small changes in key water quality parameters for specific species;

● transfer of category C or D pathogens.

For the present level of assessment, the thresholds of significance for disease transfer have been based on the presence or absence of diseases in the recipient waters. At a more detailed level, the relative incidence of certain diseases will influence the impact acceptability of a water transfer scheme. Fish disease controls are currently under review in order to meet the requirements of the EC Fish Health Directive 91/67 which came into force in January 1993. Current NRA policy with respect to restrictive actions for category B, C and D diseases may therefore be changed in the near future.

AQUATIC ECOLOGY   The complexity of aquatic ecosystems, and the lack of precise information about the influence of flows on the biota, hinders the assessment of aquatic ecological impacts. The assessments are therefore subjective although based upon experience of river regulation schemes and clear qualitative guidelines:

● All inter-basin transfers will impact the aquatic ecology of the donor and recipient rivers to some extent; attention is therefore focused on the questions of impact type and magnitude.

● Because scientific knowledge of ecosystem-level changes of aquatic systems to flow abstraction, regulation and augmentation is far from complete, the naturalness of the rivers affected is considered to be a key variable. Utilisation of artificial rivers (with artificially-influenced flows, river levels, water quality and channel form) is preferred for use. This protects 'natural' systems and, for some recipient channels, offers the possibility of enhancing the ecological value of degraded reaches.

● Because of the structure of the drainage network, impacts have been assessed at two scales: local and regional. The number of streams of each order declines geometrically with increasing order. A major (local) impact on a 1st-order stream may be only minor significance at the regional scale because there are many 1st order streams within the network. However, a major impact on a 4th order river may be significant locally and regionally because there are relatively few rivers of this size in the region.

● Following the points made above, high-order 'natural' reaches have been given particularly high value for protection.

● Impacts of hydrological change upon instream habitats depend upon the consequent changes of hydraulic conditions which relates to site-specific channel morphology (slope, width, bedform etc). In the absence of such data, hydraulic thresholds cannot be defined and impacts on specific habitats for rare species cannot be precisely evaluated.

● Ecological quality is assessed by reference to general indices Biological Monitoring Working Party (BMWP), Average Score per Taxa (ASPT), the RIVPACS model and subsequent biological banding. Again specific community characteristics have not been considered and judgement about impacts has been based upon general principles.

Other factors taken into consideration in the assessment process have included:

● large differences in RIVPACS class between the donor and recipient rivers;

● changes in the seasonality of flows;

● systematic reduction in flow below the one in ten year dry season flow;

● frequency of operation of the transfer scheme greater than once in every ten years if the donor and recipient rivers are of significantly different biochemical status.

The risk of impact is considered greatest where the affected river or canal system is of high sensitivity, quantified by high BMWP scores, high number of taxa, high ASPT and afforded biological band A.

TERRESTRIAL ECOLOGY   A highly significant adverse impact has been considered to arise where sites of international, European or national importance are affected by a scheme, i.e. RAMSAR sites, habitats listed in the European Habitats Directive, Special Protection Areas, National Nature Reserves and SSSIs. The impacts are also considered of high significance where a large number of county designated sites are affected, and where the viability of protected, rare or declining species is at risk. Some habitats which cannot be recreated, especially ancient woodland, and semi-natural habitats or river corridors which, whilst not necessarily afforded statutory designation, form an important part of the resource base, should also be taken into account.

AGRICULTURAL LAND

Although the increasing efficiency of agricultural procedures and changes in agricultural policy have reduced the priority to retain land in agricultural use (DoE Planning Policy Guidance Note 7), the Note confirms the need to conserve the best land as a long term valuable agricultural resource. MAFF guidelines indicate that a loss of more than 20 ha of grade 1, 2 or 3a land under the Agriculture Land Classification System would be a considered highly significant impact. Land of lower class is of lesser importance except where particular agricultural practices contribute to the quality of the broad rural environment, as in the Environmentally Sensitive Areas and the three Tir Cymen areas in Wales.

ARCHAEOLOGY AND CULTURAL HERITAGE

The DoE PPG Note 16 'Archaeology and Planning' (DoE, 1990) underlines the national importance of many archaeological sites and the need for their protection. Guidance on policies and procedures concerning conservation areas and listed buildings is set out in DoE Circular 8/87. Highly significant impacts are defined as those affecting World Heritage Sites, Scheduled Ancient Monuments and Grade I/II listed buildings, or a large number of other archaeological monuments of local interest.

RECREATION, AMENITY AND NAVIGATION

Highly sensitive areas in this category include lowland river or canal reaches with statutory navigation, and areas used for contact water sports. The risk of adverse impact is considered high where rapid fluctuations in flows would impede navigation, or where flows are reduced by abstraction to levels insufficient to maintain navigation depth without increased dredging. Water sports are similarly influenced by changes to the flow regime, and where appropriate water quality objectives are affected. A potential impact on visual amenity has been considered to be a moderate risk. Many of the impacts of river transfer schemes may be beneficial in this category, particularly with respect to the augmentation of low flows.

A3.5
COMPARISON OF STRATEGIC OPTIONS

Each scheme component has been assessed using data from existing reports and option studies. The results of the assessments have then been drawn together in a summary matrix for each of the strategic development options and presented in Table A3.5. The overall assessment for each option has been taken to be the sum of its components and the breakdown between construction (short term) and operation (long term) impacts and between "high" and "moderate" has been retained rather than combine the assessments in an overall index. Benefit opportunities have also been retained in the option matrix.

This approach effectively gives equal weighting to different categories of impact which means that schemes with more components have a higher likelihood of appearing to have a higher environmental risk. Clearly some impacts will be more important than others and consideration will need to be given to reflect this when comparing schemes in more detail. At this stage the matrix is intended to present information on a consistent basis rather than to directly form the basis for making decisions.

It is again stressed that this is a preliminary comparison, based on available data, and that substantial further study and investigation is required for each of these options before the NRA could be in a position to make a comprehensive assessment.

A3.6
KEY ISSUES

From the assessment of scheme specific risks and opportunities a number of general issues emerge relating to the NRA's duty to both manage resources efficiently and to protect and enhance the environment.

It is inevitable that all reservoir construction and inter-basin transfers will have some impact on the aquatic environment. The issues relate to the scale of change, i.e. local versus regional, and the significance of change, i.e. the degree of variance from the natural state.

It is generally possible to identify and mitigate issues that relate to the planning, construction and short term operational stages of schemes. However, there is insufficient information at present from which to adequately assess the long term environmental effects of changes in flow regime and quality resulting from river regulation and inter-basin transfers. No comprehensive studies exist of the impact of any large scale transfer schemes in the UK and extension of inter-basin transfers could be supported only after further investigation and study. *Therefore a precautionary approach to water resources development is required.* However, there is no inherent reason why water resources schemes cannot be built and operated without causing long term environmental deterioration given careful planning, implementation and monitoring.

While each scheme needs to be considered on its merits, those involving further regulation of already largely "artificial" rivers appear preferable to those using "natural" rivers, subject to the setting of suitable environmental standards. Indeed, new schemes could offer long term benefits, provided clear and holistic environmental objectives are incorporated at the outset.

Small scale impacts associated with the construction of pipelines, pumping stations and small storage reservoirs can generally all be overcome by careful design and route selection. The acceptability of these components is largely a matter for planning authorities.

A3.7
FURTHER STUDIES

Future study requirements identified are:

● Investigation of the environmental impacts of existing UK transfer and regulation schemes, such as Kielder; Ely Ouse-Essex; Elan Valley, Dee; and Clywedog to establish the actual positive and negative environmental impacts of such schemes in UK conditions.

● Evaluation of economic techniques for quantifying environmental damage and benefits in the context of water resources projects.

● Determination of minimum residual flow requirements in major rivers and to estuaries, particularly migratory salmonid requirements.

● Continued research into the links between terrestrial wetland sites and hydrological regimes, to establish guidelines for acceptable changes to minimum water flows/levels and frequency of flooding for different categories of site.

● Investigation of the risks of transfer of fish disease between catchments.

REFERENCE

1.   Department of Environment (1990) Planning Policy and Guidance: Archaeology and Planning (No.16) (HMSO, London)

TABLE A3.1

RIVER/CANAL FRAMEWORK FOR ASSIGNING SENSITIVITY

Category	Sensitivity		Benefit
	High	Moderate	
General Character/ Landscape	Semi-natural Unregulated channel	Modified	Potential for enhancing semi-natural and non-natural character
Water Quality	National Water Council (NWC) Class 1 River Water Quality Objective (RQO) - Water supply	NWC Class 2 or 3 RQO - Contact sport	Bring reach in to Class Improve NWC Class 4
Fisheries	Salmonids and certain species of coarse fish Commercially sensitive fishery	Flowing water cyprinids	Improve low biomass Improve poor quality fishery
Aquatic Ecology	High Biological Monitoring Working Party (BMWP) scores High Average Score Per Taxa (ASPT)	Moderate BMWP scores EQ1 = <1 Moderate ASPT	Improve low BMWP score for NWC Class Improve low ASPT
Terrestrial Ecology	Presence of internationally or nationally designated site Numerous regionally or locally designated sites Presence of protected species	Presence of regionally or locally designated site	Increase habitat diversity
Recreation/ Amenity/ Navigation	Statutory navigation Contact water sports	Non-statutory navigation Visual amenity importance	Restore/Improve derelict navigation Improve perceived low flows
General Land-use and Planning Issues	Conflict with existing land-use designations	Reduction in resource value	Potential for enhancement identified in Development Plan

TABLE A3.2

RESERVOIR AND PIPELINE FRAMEWORK FOR ASSIGNING SENSITIVITY			
Category	Sensitivity		Benefit
	High	Moderate	
General Character/ Landscape	Located in or near internationally or nationally designated area	Located in or near regionally or locally designated area	Increase and enhance landscape diversity
Water Quality	Public Water Supply reservoir	Off-line river regulation reservoir	Improve downstream dilution
Agriculture	MAFF Land Class 1, 2, 3a	Land Class 3b	Enhanced land access
Archaeology and Cultural Heritage	Presence of internationally or nationally designated site/monument/building	Presence of other archaeological artifacts/sites	Excavation and recording
Terrestrial Ecology	Presence of internationally or nationally designated sites Numerous regionally or locally designated sites Presence of protected species	Presence of regionally or locally designated sites	Increase habitat diversity
Recreation/Amenity	Presence of National Park or Area of Outstanding Natural Beauty	Presence of significant number of footpaths	Offer recreation potential
General Land-use and Planning Issues	Conflict with existing land-use designations		Potential for enhancement identified in Development Plan

TABLE A3.3

RIVER/CANAL FRAMEWORK FOR ASSESSING RISK OF SIGNIFICANT IMPACT

Category	High Risk		Moderate Risk		Mitigation
	Key Impact	Criteria	Key Impact	Criteria	
General Character/ Landscape	Reduction of natural character	Alteration of channel	Minor local impact on semi-natural channel or flood plain	Construction works in/ adjacent to channel	Environmentally sensitive design
Water Quality	Fall in NWC Class	Transfer of water of lower NWC Class	Increased frequency of algal blooms	Transfer of water of higher nutrient status	Water Treatment
	RQO parameter above threshold level for use	Dilution at Q_{95} of problems determinants	Increased saline intrusion		Setting of prescribed flow
Fisheries	Loss of freshets/spates for migratory salmonids	Inspection of with/ without annual hydrographs	Increased duration of velocities outside species preference	Outside natural variation of low flows	Use of artificial freshets
	Change in spawning grounds	Reduction in Q_{95} or MAM7 no worse than 1:10 year drought	Fish impingement on intakes		Use of fish screens and design of intakes
	Change in river "smell" for migrating fish	Similarity of donor/ recipient rivers and mass balance calcs.	Temperature changes due to mixing or reservoir releases	Dissimilarity of temperature and water quality dilution and frequency	Fisheries management policy
	Reduction in low flow/velocity	Flow reduction beyond natural variation			Variable depth of reservoir draw-off
	Fall in NWC Class or exceedence of threshold level for EIFAC parameter				Treatment of transfer water
	Transfer of species	Presence/ absence of species	Small changes to key water quality parameters (species dependent)	Risk to species	
	Transfer of pathogens (A and B categories)	Presence/absence of diseases	Transfer of pathogens (C and D categories)	Presence/absence of diseases	
Aquatic Ecology	Significant changes to macrophyte population	Similarity of donor/ recipient water quality and dilution	Moderate changes to macrophyte population	Similarity of donor/ recipient water quality and dilution	Water treatment
	Significant changes to macro- invertebrate population structure classified as Class A or of regional importance	Frequency of operation (<1:5)	Minor changes to macro- invertebrate population, or high changes to poor quality stretches (Class C and D)	Frequency of operation (>1:10)	
		Change in flow seasonality or variability from inspection of hydrographs		Small difference in RIVPACS class	
		Reduction in low flows (MAM7 or Q_{95} <1:10 drought values)			
		Large difference of RIVPACS class			
Terrestrial Ecology	Impact to or loss of nationally/ internationally designated site	Presence/ absence of sites and large change in flow regime through highly sensitive site	Impact to or loss of regionally or locally designated sites	Presence/ absence of sites and change in seasonality or variability of flow beyond natural range	Environmentally sensitive design of engineering works

TABLE A3.3 (continued)

RIVER/CANAL FRAMEWORK FOR ASSESSING RISK OF SIGNIFICANT IMPACT					
Category	High Risk		Moderate Risk		Mitigation
	Key Impact	Criteria	Key Impact	Criteria	
Recreation/Amenity Navigation	Increased frequency of dredging	Inspection of annual hydrographs for absence of or reduction to flushing flows	Reduction in visual amenity	Expert opinion	Use of artificial spates
	Impact on quality of angling				Setting of prescribed flows
	Loss of sports to floods				
	Increased frequency of failure to maintain navigable depth	Reduction in low flows below threshold to maintain navigable depth			
	Fall in RQO parameter for reach (covered under water quality)				
General Land-use and Planning Issues	Prejudicing potential/ planned land-use	Conflict with Development Plan		Partial conflict with Development Plan	Consultation and possibly compensation

TABLE A3.4

RESERVOIR AND PIPELINE FRAMEWORK FOR ASSESSING RISK OF SIGNIFICANT IMPACT					
Category	High Risk		Moderate Risk		Mitigation
	Key Impact	Criteria	Key Impact	Criteria	
General Character/ Landscape	Effect on internationally or nationally designated area	Permanent change to existing views	Effect on internationally or national designated area Effects on regionally or locally designated area	Temporary change to existing views Permanent change to existing views	Planned increase of visual diversity
Water Quality	Significant algal problems in reservoir or risk of exceeding threshold of parameter for public water supply use	Source and Strophic Status of stored/ transferred water	Anaerobic conditions in pipeline	Distance and frequency of operation	Water treatment Operational control rules
Agriculture	Significant loss of MAFF Class 1, 2 or 3a land	≥ 20 ha permanently lost	Major loss of Class 1, 2 or 3a land Temporary loss of Class 1, 2 or 3a land Significant loss of Class 3b land	< 20 ha loss ≥ 20 ha loss	Provision of compensation supplies
Archaeology and Cultural Heritage	Effect on international or nationally designated site/monument/building Effect on other archaeological monuments	Destruction or damage to site/monument/ building Destruction or damage to setting Cumulative damage to a significant number of sites	Effect on a limited number of other archaeological monuments	Destruction or damage to monument	Funded archaeological survey before development
Terrestrial Ecology	Effects on internationally designated site Effects on nationally designated site Effects on regionally designated sites Effects on protected species	Permanent destruction or damage Permanent destruction or damage Cumulative damage to a number of sites Loss of population or decrease in viability of population	Effects on internationally or nationally designated site Effects on regionally or locally designated site	Temporary destruction or damage Permanent destruction or damage	Habitat creation, revegetation
Recreation/Amenity	Effect on National Park or Area of Outstanding Natural Beauty	Impairment of aesthetic enjoyment	Footpath loss Footpath diversions of over 500m	Unmitigable or significant loss of footpaths	Creation of recreation/ amenity facilities
General Land-use and Planning Issues	Prejudicing potential/ planned land-use	Conflict with Development Plan		Partial conflict with Development Plan	Consultation and possibly compensation

Table A3.5

ENVIRONMENTAL ASSESSMENT OF STRATEGIC OPTIONS SUMMARY MATRIX

Legend: ■ High ■ Medium ▪ Low / Indicates Impact can be mitigated

Benefit Opportunities — Operation — Construction — Sensitivity — Potential Environmental Risks

Category Key:
- ∫ Fisheries and Aquatic Ecology
- ☘ Terrestrial Ecology
- ∿ Water Quality
- ⚓ Recreation/Amenity/Navigation
- ⚘ Agriculture
- ☂ Community Impacts
- 🏛 Archaeology and Cultural Heritage
- 🏞 General Landscape Character and Other General Planning Issues

Demand Centre	Options/Components
Thames	**Wye/Severn – Thames Transfer**
	Core Components
	Pipeline Deerhurst – Down Ampney Gravel Pits
	Restored Thames & Severn Canal
	River Thames Buscot-Egham
	Variable Components
	Unsupported - Severn d/s of Deerhurst
	Enlarged Craig Goch Reservoir
	Regulated Severn to Deerhurst
	Regulated Upper Wye to Ross
	Pipeline Ross- Deerhurst
	River Vyrnwy regulated by redeployed Vyrnwy Reservoir
	Regulated Severn to Deerhurst
	S.W. Oxfordshire Reservoir
	South West Oxfordshire Reservoir
	River Thames Culham-Egham
	BWB Canal Transfer
	Pipeline Coalport-River Penk
	River Penk to River Sow Confluence
	River Sow to Heywood Junction
	BWB Canals: Heywood Jct.-Isis Lock
	River Thames d/s of Oxford Canal
East Midlands	**Severn Trent Transfer**
	Pipeline Coalport- River Penk
	River Penk to River Sow Confluence
	River Sow to River Trent
	River Trent d/s of Great Heywood
Anglian	**Great Bradley Reservoir**
	Great Bradley Reservoir
	Tidal Ely Ouse,/Wash
	River Stour
	River Pant/Blackwater
	Unsupported Trent to Essex transfer
	Trent d/s of Torksey
	River Witham
	Pipeline Witham to Ely Ouse
	River Stour
	River Pant/Blackwater

APPENDIX 4: SUMMARY OF RESEARCH & DEVELOPMENT PROJECTS RELATING TO ENVIRONMENTAL ECONOMICS

A Summary of NRA sponsored R&D relating to environmental economics is as follows:

● **Project 052: Comparison of Charging Practices for Effluents in Three EC Member States**
The report compares charging systems operating in France, Germany and the Netherlands which have differing degrees of incentive charging. May 1990.

● **Project 248: Economic Effects of Water Resource Management**
This study involves the examination of the potential use of economic instruments for resource management purpose, with particular consideration being given to incentive pricing (or full cost pricing) and tradeable permit systems. R&D Note 128, June 1993.

● **Project 253: Econmic Value of Changes to the Water Environment**
This report provides a summary of many of the principles underlying economic analsis, identifies some of the key issues in applying economics to the environment, and reviews the different techniques available for valuation of environmental costs and benefits. R&D Note 37, January 1993.

● **Project 310: New Style Charging Schemes for Discharges and Abstractions**
The report provides an overview of the use of economic instruments (tradeable permits or incentive charges) in the regulation of abstractions from and discharges to controlled water. R&D Note 16, 1991.

● **Project 401: Evaluation of the Costs and Benefits of Low Flow Alleviation.**
The aims of this study are to provide a methodology for the economic evaluation of low flow allevaluation schemes, and to test the methodology at specific locations. The methodology is currently under review and further work involving its application to at least two locations is nearing completion. R&D Note 89, May 1992 and R&D Note 136, December 1992.

● **NRA Fellowship**
The research being undertaken under the Fellowship involves developing an economic model for the sustainable management of water resources. The Fellowship is jointly funded with the Economic and Social Research Council (ESRC) and based at the Centre for Social and Economic Reseach on the Global Environment (CSERGE).

● **Project 435: Economic Appraisal of Non-grant Aided Flood Defence Schemes**
To develop a robust method for evaluating the benefits from small non-grant aided schemes.

● **Project 468: Benefit Assessments for Water Quality Improvements**
To develop an economic benefit methodology for evaluating environmental benefits resulting from changes in water quality stemming from improvements in effluent quality and to produce a manual for practitioners.

GLOSSARY OF TERMS

1 : 50 year Drought	A drought which is likely to occur on average once every 50 years.
£M	Million Pounds Sterling
£K	Thousand Pounds Sterling
'000Ml/d	Thousand Megalitres per day
AMP2	Second Asset Management Plan - initiated by OFWAT as part of the periodic review of K adjustment.
Abstraction	The removal of water from any source, either permanently or temporarily.
Abstraction Licence	An authorisation granted by the NRA to allow the removal of water from a source of supply.
ASPT	Average score per taxa
Aquifer	A porous water bearing underground formation of permeable rock, sand or gravel capable of holding significant quantities of water.
Artificial Recharge	The filling or recharging of an aquifer by means of other than natural infiltration of precipitation and runoff
BMWP	Biological monitoring working party
BW	British Waterways
Brundtland Report	Report of the 1987 World Commission on Environment and Development.
Catchment	The area from which precipitation and groundwater will collect and contribute to the flow of a specific river.
CBI	Confederation of British Industry
Confined Aquifer	An aquifer overlain by impervious or almost impervious formation.
Conjunctive Use	Combined use of different sources of water.
CSERGE	Centre for Social and Economic Research on the Global Environment
DoE	Department of Environment
Demand Centre	A discrete area of public water supply demand in which specific sources of supply can be used to meet demand throughout that area.
Demand Management	The management of the total quantity of water abstracted from a source of supply using measures to control waste and consumption.
Direct re-use	Connection from a sewage treatment plant directly into a water treatment plant.
Discharge Consent	A licence granted by the NRA to discharge effluent of specified quality and volume.

Drift	A geological formation composed of fragmented or particulate material.
Ecology	The study of the relationship between living systems and their environment.
Effluent	Liquid waste from industrial, agricultural or sewage plants.
EIA	Environmental Impact Assessment
EIFAC	European Inland Fisheries Advisory Commission
ESRC	Economic and Social Research Council
ha	Hectare
Habitat	The customary and characteristic dwelling place of a species or community.
Hydrology	The study of water on and below the earth's surface.
Groundwater	Water held in aquifers.
l/h/d	Litres per head per day. (This is a way of expressing per capita consumption).
l/prop/day	Litres per property per day (rate of use).
l/prop/day/yr	Litres per property per day per year (change in the rate of use).
London Basin	A particular geological formation beneath the London area.
Ml/a	Megalitres per annum (one Megalitre is equal to 1 million litres or approximately 220,000 gallons).
Ml/d	Megalitres per day (one Megalitre is equal to 1 million litres or approximately 220,000 gallons)
MAFF	Ministry of Agriculture, Fisheries and Food
MAM7	Mean annual minimum 7 day flow.
mAOD	Meters above ordnance datum.
Marginal Demand	A forecast demand for public water supply which cannot be met from existing resources or new local resources which can be developed.
NRA	National Rivers Authority
NPC	Net Present Cost - the total cost of future expenditure discounted to present values.
NWC	National Water Council
OFWAT	Office of Water Services
Operating Cost	The cost of running a water resource scheme on a day to day basis.
Outage	The loss of public water supply source yields due to planned or un-planned maintenance and the permanent or temporary loss of supply due to pollution.

PCC	Per Capita Consumption or the quantity of water used for normal household domestic purposes expressed as a volume per person.
PF	Prescribed Flow - the flow which is used to control abstractions to prevent adverse impact on other users, the environment or water quality.
Precautionary Principle	Where significant environmental damage may occur, but knowledge on the matter is incomplete, decisions made and measures implemented should err on the side of caution.
PWS	Public water supply
Per Annum	Per year
Q_{95}	The flow of a river which is exceeded on average for 95% of the year.
RQO	River quality objective
RAMSAR	An international convention originally agreed in 1975 to stem the progressive encroachment on, and loss of, wetlands.
RIVPACS	River Invertebrate Prediction and Classification System
Regulated River	A river where the flow is augmented through the addition of water from another source.
SEA	Strategic Environmental Assessment
SPA	Special Protection Area
SPL	Supply Pipe Leakage
SSSI	Site of Special Scientific Interest
Sewage	Liquid waste from cities, towns and villages which is conveyed in sewers.
Surface Water	Water which flows or is stored on the ground surface.
Sustainable Development	Development that meets the needs of the present without compromising the ability of future generations to meet their own needs.
Total Treated Water Losses	The sum total of the loss of water from water company distribution systems, customer supply pipes and general domestic leakage.
Wetland	An area of low lying land where the water table is at or near the surface for most of the time leading to characteristic habitats.
Yield	The reliable rate at which water can be drawn from a water resource.

The National Rivers Authority